"I have read and heard preached a ton on the reality that 'all of life is worship.' It is, and I wouldn't want to dispute that point. But what about when the covenant people of God gather together? Are there not some ways God desires us to worship corporately that can differ from how we worship in 'all of life'? Mike Cosper has served the church well with *Rhythms of Grace*. I was both convicted and compelled as I read it."

Matt Chandler, Lead Pastor, The Village Church; President, Acts 29 Church Planting Network

"Mike Cosper is uniquely gifted as both a musician and a pastor to speak into the culture where art and church meet and mesh. This is an important book for folks thinking about what it is to be a musician, a worship leader, and everything in between. The historic question of how we worship on Sunday and with our lives is an important one to keep asking because the songs we sing have the power to shape who we are and who we will become as individuals and as a community."

Sandra McCracken, singer-songwriter

"Years ago, A. W. Tozer remarked that worship was the missing jewel of the evangelical church. Since that time, evangelicals have been engaged in an urgent and sometimes feverish struggle to determine the nature of true biblical worship. In *Rhythms of Grace*, Mike Cosper takes us back to first principles and roots his understanding of worship deeply within the context of the Christian gospel. This is a book that will offer much to Christians and church leaders seeking to understand worship. It is both biblical and deeply practical, and it is written by an author who has deep experience in the worship life of a thriving and faithful congregation."

R. Albert Mohler Jr., President, The Southern Baptist Theological Seminary

"Reading Mike's *Rhythms of Grace* was like sitting across the table from someone you need to be listening to. In this season of the church, there is some confusion on what a worship leader is and does, and why. This book brings great clarity to those questions. As someone who aims to see song leaders become worship leaders and worship leaders become worship pastors, I found this to be a key resource. This will be an important text in training new leaders, and a great reminder to more seasoned leaders, to sing the gospel and, above all, highlight Jesus."

Charlie Hall, Worship and Arts Director, Frontline Church, Oklahoma City

"I know of no one more insightful on questions of worship than Mike Cosper, and I know of no one more gifted to articulate a Christ-focused, kingdom-directed, Spirit-driven sense of what it means to worship in the presence of the triune God. Read this book and see if it does not drive you to repattern your worship to fit the full rejoicing, lamenting, raging force of biblical adoration of God."

Russell D. Moore, Dean, The Southern Baptist Theological Seminary

"When Mike Cosper writes, I read. And even though I'm not a pastor and don't play the guitar, I learned a lot from him about how the gospel of grace shapes our rhythms of congregational worship. Pick up this book and benefit from his biblical wisdom and pastoral experience."

Collin Hansen, Editorial Director, The Gospel Coalition; coauthor, *A God-Sized Vision: Revival Stories That Stretch and Stir*

"This book challenges worship leaders not merely to announce a gospel of grace in Jesus Christ, but also to begin to discover how that gospel reshapes every dimension and element of worship. It invites readers into a world where theology and practice, belief and action are intimately intertwined—where every practice reflects and then reinforces a theological vision, and every doctrine both grounds and sharpens practices. Who better to offer this challenge and invitation than a reflective practitioner who considers it a joy to discern the implications of this gospel of grace for a host of practical concerns, week-by-week, year-by-year?"

John D. Witvliet, Director, Calvin Institute of Christian Worship; Professor of Worship, Theology, and Congregational and Ministry Studies, Calvin College and Calvin Theological Seminary

"We don't need another book telling us how to do worship to grow our church or connect with our culture. We need historical rootedness, not contemporary fads. We need to be taught so that we can teach the church to worship along with the story line of the gospel."

Darrin Patrick, Lead Pastor, The Journey, St. Louis; author, *For the City* and *Church Planter: The Man, The Message, The Mission*

"I can't overstate my excitement about Mike Cosper's new book *Rhythms of Grace*. This practical volume represents the many years my good friend has spent in serious theological reflection, doxological engagement, and faithful service in the body of Christ—at Sojourn Church and well beyond. Mike's passion for God's glory and God's worship are evident on every page. In particular, I'm thankful for how Mike helps us plan our services of worship in light of the history of redemption and the riches of God's grace. Liturgy isn't a four-letter word; it's the storyboard that helps us connect with God's commitment to redeem people, places, and things through the person and work of Jesus. I will use Mike's tremendous book in the seminary classes I teach on worship; but I will also place it in the hands of seasoned worship leaders and young congregants alike. Thanks, dear brother, for your art and heart!"

Scotty Smith, Founding Pastor, Christ Community Church, Franklin, Tennessee

"The greatest composers are gifted synthesizers. They have the ability to weave what they've heard and learned and experienced in the past into their own musical stories. If *Rhythms of Grace* were a symphony, the critics would hail it as a masterful work of synthesis—a fusion of biblical, historical, cultural, and philosophical elements into an engaging, challenging, and thoughtful treatment of worship. At the end of this work, you'll also be able to sing the primary thematic motif—the gospel of Jesus Christ."

Joseph Crider, Senior Associate Dean, School of Church Ministries, The Southern Baptist Theological Seminary

"For the glory and enjoyment of God, the health of the church, and the spread of the gospel—this is why you should read *Rhythms of Grace* by Mike Cosper. In this book Mike proves to be a good pastor, giving us a practical theology of worship that cautions against and corrects error, while shepherding us toward a more biblically faithful understanding and experience of worship in the church gathered and scattered."

Joe Thorn, author, *Note to Self: The Discipline of Preaching to Yourself*; Lead Pastor, Redeemer Fellowship, St. Charles, Illinois

"An important contribution to the discussion among many younger evangelicals about worship and liturgy. Mike writes with grace, and with wisdom beyond his years. Frankly, I am amazed by the amount of ground he manages to cover! Mike introduces us to ideas and thinkers that we all in the evangelical world should know. He has set a lofty goal, painting a picture of liturgy as a beautiful way, and I believe he succeeds. For anyone nervous about exploring the world of liturgy, Mike is a gentle and wise companion."

Kevin Twit, Campus Minister, RUF; Founder, Indelible Grace Music

"Mike Cosper has written a book that is both easily accessible and deeply challenging for all who want to see worship flourish in their congregations. *Rhythms of Grace* is a must read—especially for church musicians and pastors who desire to deepen their understanding of how worship shapes and forms individuals and communities."

Isaac Wardell, Founder, Bifrost Arts

"For many churches, a well-thought-out approach to how to lead music is woefully lacking. This needs to change, and this book will surely help. *Rhythms of Grace* is a book I will rely on in the future to develop music leaders for our church and the churches we plant. Clear, beautifully written, theologically grounded, and yet very practically helpful and completely gospel-centered—this is a book for pastors and music leaders alike. In fact, I would get two copies so that pastors and musicians can read it together!"

Zach Nielson, Pastor, The Vine Church, Madison, Wisconsin

RHYTHMS
OF
GRACE

HOW THE CHURCH'S *Worship* TELLS
THE STORY OF THE GOSPEL

MIKE COSPER

FOREWORD BY BOB KAUFLIN

:: CROSSWAY

WHEATON, ILLINOIS

Rhythms of Grace: How the Church's Worship Tells the Story of the Gospel

Copyright © 2013 by Mike Cosper

Published by Crossway
      1300 Crescent Street
      Wheaton, Illinois 60187

Cover design: Tyler Deeb, Pedale Design

First printing 2013

Printed in the United States of America

Unless otherwise indicated, Scripture quotations are from the ESV® Bible (*The Holy Bible, English Standard Version*®), copyright © 2001 by Crossway. 2011 Text Edition. Used by permission. All rights reserved.

Scripture references marked NIV are taken from The Holy Bible, New International Version®, NIV®. Copyright © 1973, 1978, 1984, 2011 by Biblica, Inc.™ Used by permission. All rights reserved worldwide.

Scripture references marked NIV84 are taken from The Holy Bible, New International Version®, NIV®. Copyright © 1973, 1978, 1984 by Biblica, Inc.™ Used by permission. All rights reserved worldwide.

Emphasis in Scripture quotations has been added by the author.

Trade paperback ISBN: 978-1-4335-3342-6
Mobipocket ISBN: 978-1-4335-3344-0
PDF ISBN: 978-1-4335-3343-3
ePub ISBN: 978-1-4335-3345-7

Library of Congress Cataloging-in-Publication Data

Cosper, Mike, 1980–
    Rhythms of grace : how the church's worship tells the story of the gospel / Mike Cosper.
       pages cm
    Includes bibliographical references (pages) and indexes.
    ISBN 978-1-4335-3342-6 (tp)
    1. Worship. I. Title.
BV10.3.C67   2013
264—dc23   2012040115

Crossway is a publishing ministry of Good News Publishers.

VP		23	22	21	20	19	18	17	16	15	14	13
15	14	13	12	11	10	9	8	7	6	5	4	3	2	1

To the memory of Chip Stam,
who in both life and death
displayed the glories of Jesus,
and who taught me almost
everything I know that's
worth saying.

CONTENTS

FOREWORD

The first time I heard the title of Mike Cosper's book, I wondered if he couldn't have come up with something a little catchier.

Rhythms of Grace. What does that even mean? A manual on using percussion for the glory of God? Maybe a Christian version of *Dancing with the Stars*?

Actually, I'd enjoy reading Mike's thoughts on either of those topics, because he's a superb writer. But the subtitle clears up any confusion. *How the Church's Worship Tells the Story of the Gospel.*

I've known Mike Cosper for about ten years now. And of all the things I appreciate about him and his work with Sojourn Music, this tops the list: Mike Cosper is a gospel-saturated man. It's why even though we come from very different backgrounds and I'm old enough to be his dad, I've come to count him as a dear friend. Mike doesn't merely use the word *gospel* as an add-on adjective to impress people. He expounds on it, explains it, rehearses it, celebrates it. He approaches his life, his marriage, his family, his church, and his world in view of the gospel: Jesus's perfect life, atoning death, and victorious resurrection. And he carries a deep and relentless burden that others would do the same.

And that's why he wrote *Rhythms of Grace*. He explains it like this:

> [Congregational] worship is an invitation to step into the rhythms of grace. We remember our identity as gospel-formed people, journeying together through the story that gave us our identity and being sent out to live gospel-shaped lives. Practiced in these rhythms, we learn to think in them, much as we learn to improvise on an instrument.

If you're a musician like me, you get the necessity of repetition. I spent four years pursuing a piano performance degree, practicing at times up to ten hours a day. My goal was to be proficient enough at the end of college to play anything I wanted to. Not a very God-glorifying goal, but clear and simple.

I immersed myself daily in the mechanics of technique, scales, arpeggios. I gave dogged attention to the details of dynamics, tempo, pedaling, and style. In the end, it set me free to actually make music. And it wasn't always simply reproducing notes on a page. My practice helped me stretch out beyond printed music to create melodies, harmonies, and rhythms on my own. But they were all rooted in the knowledge of music I had gained in the practice room.

Rhythms of Grace is largely an apologetic for repetition, but its effects and ends are far more transcendent than learning how to improvise on the piano. It teaches us how to live before a holy and gracious God in light of the gospel, and how our meetings can serve that end.

In an engaging, compelling, and creative way, Mike traces the story of grace God has been weaving since before the dawn of time. It's a story filled with hope, tragedy, conquest, defeat, desperation, beauty, pain, and inexpressible glory. It's the most important story that will ever be told. And it's a story we are easily and quickly prone to forget.

Mike takes our hand and skillfully walks us through that story, from the garden of Eden, through the wilderness, through Israel's checkered history, until we finally arrive at the point of the story, Jesus. At numerous times I was caught up in the utter brilliance and sheer beauty of God's sovereign plan of redemption.

Mike goes on to review the relative success of the church in continuing the gospel story. The final chapters are devoted to unpacking the practical implications of all this for our participation and leadership in the church today. Along the way, Mike winsomely but firmly addresses things like avoiding common errors we've made, choosing musical styles, and developing a gospel-informed liturgy.

While you may not agree with every conclusion he comes to (I didn't!), I have no doubt that, like me, you'll benefit immensely

from the thoughtful way he addresses each issue. Most impor-
tantly, you'll come away with a clearer understanding of why the
good news of Jesus Christ must shape, inform, govern, inspire,
and fill our weekly gatherings.

There's a chance some of you might be put off by Mike's references to liturgy, that is, the order of events in the public meetings of the church. You may remember as a kid enduring years
of weekly services that seemed dull, cold, and lifeless. And you're
not about to give yourself to it again.

No worries. In his typical grace-filled and pastoral way, Mike
helps us understand the difference between liturgical practices
that seek to earn God's acceptance and liturgies that are whole-
hearted responses to God's grace in Christ. He reminds us of the
humble and ennobling effect of identifying with Christians who
have gone faithfully before us.

Apart from the content of *Rhythms of Grace*, which I can't com-
mend highly enough, Mike's writing style is eminently enjoyable.
He not only helps us see what is most important, but does it in a
way that is accessible, imaginative, and beautiful.

I'm glad you'll be reading this book. If you read it carefully,
I don't think you'll ever view Sundays the same way again. As
Mike says:

> Gathering for worship is a life-shaping moment in a congrega-
> tion's week, and our task as pastors is to seize that opportunity
> for an all-out assault on their hearts. As servants of God, we
> prepare people for death, and we prepare them for eternity. And
> most of them just think they're "going to church."

May none of us ever think we are just "going to church." My
prayer is that God would use this book to open your eyes wider
to the glories of the gospel and the opportunity we have every
week as the church of Jesus Christ to grow deeper in the grace
and knowledge of Jesus Christ.

Bob Kauflin
Louisville, Kentucky

PREFACE

I didn't set out to be a worship pastor. As with many pastors and worship leaders I know, it was sort of a happy accident. In the fall of 1999, I had big dreams of stardom. I wanted to be a record producer or a rock star. I was also a serious Christian, about to get married, and gathering regularly with a small group of wandering Christians in a Louisville apartment. We were all feeling disenfranchised from our home churches and were praying about what God would have us do next.

A mutual friend connected our prayer group with Daniel Montgomery, a seminary student who wanted to plant a church in our neighborhood, and a partnership was formed. A big chunk of our prayer group joined the core of the church, and in September 2000, Sojourn Community Church was born.

In the years prior to this, I'd led bands for a variety of youth and worship ministries, and so I was asked to serve as the co-ordinator for Sojourn's music ministry. Very soon this role took on a feeling of calling. I came on staff about a year later. I began learning the ropes of pastoring, preparing worship services, and working with artists. Fast forward a few years, and I'm a pastor. No one was more surprised than I.

A Growing Trend

I think my story isn't that uncommon, especially among the many young churches and church plants across the nation. Gifted musicians, eager to serve, find themselves stumbling into roles of leadership. Singer-songwriters and would-be rock stars fit the mold for worship leaders that has become a cultural norm and end up shaping the worship practices of congregations.

On the one hand, it has the potential to be a good thing. It's grass-roots leadership, emerging from a local context and shaping the church's culture. On the other, it's fraught with challenges. Worship pastors with little to no formal training are like boats adrift, trying to figure out what worship really is about, how it's best led and cultivated, and how it connects to Scripture, history, and the culture around us.

I was blessed with mentors and wise counselors who steered me in the direction of good resources, good thinking, and good shepherding. Many others aren't so lucky. Instead, they find themselves shaped by a culture of worship that's enmeshed with a culture of celebrity and consumerism. Worship leaders, it's believed, should be entertainers and performers, musicians with cool haircuts and wild song arrangements that dazzle and thrill. The task of preparing to gather with God's people is shaped by an insatiable and consumeristic need for the new and the cutting-edge. The short life cycle of worship songs today—hip today, gone tomorrow—is a clear symptom of a consumer society's shaping influence on the church.

I don't blame worship leaders. It's hard to blame anyone, really. These realities are utterly pervasive, and their impact occurs without anyone intending it. No one decides to be consumeristic. No one decides to embrace a celebrity culture or consumer attitude, but mass culture has a way of swallowing people and institutions whole, and one day you wake up wondering, "How did we get here?"

Asking Why?

I remember a particular moment, sometime in the first year or two of the church, when I found myself feeling particularly lost. I was off the platform that week, running sound in the back of the old, stone-walled church where Sojourn gathered. It was early in the life of our church plant, and the music was usually a rowdy, indie-rock affair, ringing off the limestone and stained glass and encompassing the young congregation of 150 or so who peppered the pews. Though we weren't the most expressive church at the time (timid to sing out or raise hands), this service in particular was going well, and the people were as enthused as they ever got during a gathering.

Suddenly I thought, "How on earth did we get here?" I wasn't thinking about the building we rented or the church that was gathered. I was thinking much more broadly. The early church didn't have drums and guitars, and probably never saw anything like the "worship leaders" that were a standard presence in the churches I'd attended since I was a kid. Where did all of this come from?

It wasn't a foreboding feeling. I didn't think that we were playing with "strange fire" and doomed to condemnation, but I was suddenly aware of my own cluelessness. Why did we gather? Why did we sing? Why did we do it the way we did?

The *why* haunted me. Maybe there was a better way.

Our service had a general order like many churches'. We played fast songs to start the service, slower songs right before the sermon, and reversed the order at the end—slower songs leading to fast songs to send everyone out. I'd never considered why we did it that way. A worship service, I assumed, was worship (which meant music) and preaching.

Asking *why* about worship sent me on a long journey. It's tempting, when you begin to question why the church gathers, to get very discouraged by all that's problematic with worship culture. Celebrity pastors and worship leaders are everywhere, leading services that seem more about spectacle than substance. Some react to that culture by moralizing the value of the small, the local, the "organic." When you're disgusted by celebrity, the house church seems very alluring.

Along with some other pastors at Sojourn, I searched high and low, sitting at the feet of spiritual-formation gurus, learning from house-church movements, combing through book after book about the "emerging" church, and reading the critiques and responses to that movement. The fads and hype piled up around us, and our despair grew. The search for clarity about what it meant to be the church and why we gathered only made the answers cloudier.

Somehow, the story of the gospel broke through the confusion.[1] In the churches where I'd grown up, the gospel was often treated as peripheral—the gateway to Christianity, but not central to ordinary Christian life. You deal with the gospel when you become a Christian, and then you move on to bigger things as you mature.

Like Christians throughout the centuries, the other pastors and I discovered that the gospel is far more than an entrance exam or a gateway; it is the center point for all of the Christian life. This story is the defining fact for all of our past, present, and future, and we needed to live and worship with that in mind.

"You know," I thought, "if the gospel is supposed to be central to the Christian life, we should craft our worship services in such a way that they rehearse that story. Every week, we should gather and remember that God is holy, we are sinners, and Jesus saves us from our sins. We could do it with Scripture readings and songs and sermons and the Lord's Supper. Every week is an opportunity to reorient ourselves around the greater story of creation, fall, redemption, and consummation." I thought I was brilliant and innovative. In truth, I was only rediscovering what many generations of Christians had discovered long, long before.

Worship as Gospel Remembrance

If you look at almost any historical worship service or worship order, you'll find that all basically engage in the same dialogue; they all rehearse the gospel story. There is plenty of variation in the details or in the degree of clarity, but the dialogue is generally the same. God is holy. We are sinners. Jesus saves us from our sins. We gather, remember our identity-shaping story, and

---

[1] I talk much more about this journey and the "discovery" of the gospel in *Faithmapping*, which I wrote with Daniel Montgomery, our lead pastor.

send one another back into the wider world, allowing that story to shape us as we go.

It's a rhythm of life, forming our identity as a gospel-shaped people. It's a gospel rhythm, reminding us of our dependence and Christ's sufficiency. It's a rhythm of grace, spurring us on to live in the life-giving outpouring of love and mercy from the God of the universe.

Soon after rediscovering the gospel, my colleagues and I rediscovered these rhythms of grace. We began to see how the story shapes the community, and the movements of gathering and sending continue to tell the story as the church lives out its mission in the wider world. Recognizing this revolutionized church, worship, and mission for us because we saw the gospel clearly at the center. It also changed the way we saw worship. The gospel was actually all about worship, once broken by sin, now restored in Jesus. Worship, too, was all about the gospel, rehearsing the story and allowing it to shape the lives of the worshiping church.

In the pages that follow, I want to retrace that story in broad strokes. In chapters 1–4, I want to revisit creation, fall, and redemption with an eye toward how worship shifts and changes from Eden (chap. 1), to the wilderness (chap. 2), to Israel (chap. 3), to Jesus (chap. 4). From there, I want to look at where we are now (chap. 5, "Worship One, Two, Three") and what the goal of the gathering is (chap. 6, "Worship as Spiritual Formation"). Chapter 7, on the rhythms of grace, is a walk through the practices the church has engaged in historically when it has gathered; this chapter explores both how we can engage in those same practices when we gather and how they shape life when we scatter out into the world. Chapter 8, "Liturgy and the Rhythms of Grace," is about the parts of a worship service and how they work together. Chapter 9 deals with the importance of singing and some of the challenges that come with contemporary music in the gathered church. Finally, chapter 10, "The Pastoral Worship Leader," looks at worship leading as a pastoral calling, exploring it through the life and work of Isaac Watts.

It's my hope that this book will benefit a variety of folks. I've written it with the desire to help pastors, worship leaders, volunteers in worship ministries, and ordinary churchgoing worshipers participate in worship with more clarity and intentionality. There's a lot of talk about gospel-centered ministry these days, and sometimes that can feel like a rubber stamp. I hope to actually show in some detail the connection between the gospel and worship, and to talk very practically about how that can get worked out in the gatherings of the church.

What I'm Leaving Out

There are certain issues I've chosen to either give minimal detail or leave out entirely. My intention here is to introduce some ideas about the story of worship and the church. Mostly I'm telling that story from about a fifty-thousand-foot elevation, and my hope is that if something strikes your interest, you'll dig into it further.

Preaching, Communion, and baptism, for instance, could have consumed this entire book, and while there is no doubt in my mind that these are crucial issues for worship in the local church, here I want to spend more energy emphasizing the story of worship and the broader purposes of the gathering. Within the broad framework that I'll lay out, preaching, Communion, and baptism all have their places, and I think that will be clear.

I don't deal much with church governance or ecclesiology either. Various traditions have various rules governing how they worship and how they plan worship, and I don't intend to take on any of those structures in this book. Instead, I want to point to the practices that most traditions share to one degree or another and see how the gospel informs them, even as the practices form and shape us.[2]

I'm also staying away from the debates about the regulative principle and the normative principle. If you're unfamiliar with

---

[2] For the record, I'm a Protestant, Reformed Baptist, in a strongly Free Church tradition, and I write from that vantage point. Nonetheless, I think there is much common ground among evangelicals because most of the church's worship practices are centered on the story of the gospel.

these terms, they involve a long-standing debate about what the church should and shouldn't do when it gathers, according to Scripture. While I'm sympathetic to the regulative principle in principle (no pun intended), I agree with Mark Driscoll, who said the phrase "has been so widely abused, misused and misrepresented, it is not a very helpful term any longer."[3] The debates around it are complex and exhausting, and I didn't want to dive into the details here.[4] New Testament theologian D. A. Carson has said, "For all their differences, theologically rich and serious services from both camps often have more common content than either side usually acknowledges."[5] With that in mind, I think most of what I have to say here can apply to either camp.

A Note on Language

One final caveat on the word *worship*. I go to some effort here to make clear that worship is both an all-of-life, "scattered" reality and a uniquely communal, "gathered" reality. I also make a significant effort to clarify that Jesus is our one true worship leader. With that said, I think it's okay to use the words *worship* and *worship leader* when talking about a service for the gathered church and those who lead such a service. Though this may drive some of you crazy, that's certainly not my intention.

---

[3] Driscoll, *Religion Saves*, 256.
[4] D. A. Carson's discussion of it in "Worship under the Word," chapter 1 of *Worship by the Book*, is very helpful, as is Driscoll's chapter on the topic in *Religion Saves*.
[5] Carson, *Worship by the Book*, 55.

ACKNOWLEDGMENTS

My wife, Sarah, is always subjected to my thoughts and questions before anyone else is, and she graciously tolerates my angst as I work through any project or idea.

I feel blessed to have been in Sojourn Community Church and in Louisville for all these years. My pastor and friend, Daniel Montgomery, has been encouraging, challenging, and liberating as I've explored, experimented, tried, and failed while building a worship ministry at Sojourn. Rob Plummer, one of Sojourn's elders and a true friend, has wrestled with me at many points here in this book.

I'm certain I wouldn't have devoted my adult life to the worshiping church if it weren't for Mike Frazier, who pulled me into a music ministry when I was just a fifteen-year-old kid.

I am extremely thankful for the help Sarah Galyon gave with organizing my research and notes from years of note-taking, teaching, and training sessions. Likewise, Erika St. Clair has given many hours to helping annotate and organize the manuscript.

There are many men whom I count as mentors and teachers, both personally and from a distance. John Witvliet and the Calvin Institute for Christian Worship have been a steady source of learning and blessing. Isaac Wardell, Bruce Benedict, Kevin Twit, Harold Best, and Bob Kauflin have been faithful friends and guides.

Most of all, I am deeply thankful for the friendship, rebukes, and spurring of Chip Stam, without whom I would never have met these other men. For the better part of ten years, I could count on Chip's presence as a constructive critic and a faithful model for what it meant to be a pastor of worship. Witvliet once wrote that the job of a worship pastor is to prepare the congregation for their encounter with death. Chip modeled that in his life, leading worship that pointed to the sufficiency of Christ and the hope of the resurrection, and he modeled it in his death. While his cancer-ravaged body withered away, his confidence and hope shined like a beacon. I can say with no exaggeration that I am eternally grateful.

Chapter 1

THE SONG OF EDEN

The gospel is a story about worship. It begins with promise and serenity, spins wildly and terribly off course, and is rescued in the most unexpected and surprising way possible. I want to tell that story.

Worship as Story

I want to tell it because I think we don't get it. When we say the word *worship*, a lot of activity comes to mind—singing, reading the Scriptures, preaching, praying, celebrating baptism and the Lord's Supper—but we often see those practices as ends in themselves. Doing so defines worship in our minds as merely a list of things that we *do* even if we aren't certain about why we do them. They become empty duties, and we start to believe that it's necessary to do them to earn God's favor. Worship then becomes associated with religiosity—a belief that good behavior qualifies us for membership in God's family. We begin to doubt our standing before God any time we miss a worship service, or we don't participate enthusiastically, or we don't identify emotionally with the content of the songs, prayers, and sermons. Obviously, we just need to try harder and get it right at the next gathering.

Or do we? The story of worship as told in the Bible defines worship in a radically different and surprising way. It's a story that surprises us because we discover that it doesn't primarily feature us. The star of the story is God, who is at the center of all worship but is also at its origins in history and its origins in our hearts. The story of worship (like the story of the gospel) is all about God.

I want to tell that story because I believe it will reinvigorate our passion for worship and for all the activities we normally associate with it. The gospel story *is* the worship story. Worship was God's idea as he initiated creation. Just when it looked as though sin had corrupted worship beyond repair, he rescued it by sending his Son and making a way through him to worship the Father again. The Son, in turn, sent his Spirit, who awakened corpses like you and me and put a song in our hearts that we'll be singing with every breath from here to eternity.

So buckle up. Let's dive into the story of worship, which is to say, let's dive into the story of the gospel. Because the gospel is all about worship.

Before the Foundations of the World

When we think about the beginning of the gospel story, we tend to think Genesis 1. There the author brings us to the explosive moment when God spoke creation into existence. It's a good place to begin, for sure, but perhaps we should start in the moments before then. To even imagine that, we can hear the words from the Gospel of John, where the apostle tells us that before the dawning of creation, there was the loving community of the Trinity (see John 1:1; 17:24).

So before the world began, there was love. It flowed—perfect, complete, and constant—between the three persons of the Trinity. This love was an unending appreciation, a perpetual beholding and rejoicing in the goodness and perfection of the Father, Son, and Holy Spirit. The scene was what theologian Fred Sanders calls the "happy land of the Trinity."[1] It was, and is, a totally self-sufficient community of love and glory.

At its heart, worship is rooted in this love. The Trinitarian community is, in a sense, perpetually beholding one another with love and amazement. We're able to peek through the windows on that love in the Bible, where we see the Son worship the Father,

---

[1] Sanders, *The Deep Things of God*, 81.

the Father adore and exalt the Son, and the Spirit being both cel-ebrated and celebrating the others. The word *worship* comes from the Old English *weorthscipe*, which combines two words meaning "ascribe worth." The Trinity can be said to be always at worship because the three persons of the Godhead perfectly behold the worth and wonder of one another.

To our imaginations, it's probably strange (at the least) or gross (at the worst) to envision anyone perpetually exalting himself. We live in a world full of bluster and bragging, where Nicki Minaj boasts "I'm the best," LeBron James tattoos "Chosen 1" across his shoulders, and everyone from pastors to porn stars are self-celebrating on Twitter and Facebook. The idea that God would be associated with anything like that behavior is disconcerting.

But God's own self-adoration is nothing like ours. Unlike our own self-congratulatory spirit, God's view of himself is unmis-taken and unexaggerated. As hymn writer Fredrick Lehman said:

> Could we with ink the ocean fill,
> And were the skies of parchment made,
> Were every stalk on earth a quill,
> And every man a scribe by trade,
> To write the love of God above,
> Would drain the ocean dry.
> Nor could the scroll contain the whole,
> Though stretched from sky to sky.[2]

God's glory and perfection are inexhaustible. We can't say enough about how glorious he truly is. The greatest gift he can give us is a revelation of himself. Exalting anything else would be cruel.

Creation: God's Overflowing Love

It's out of the overflow of this endless love that God created the world. The whole Trinity is present at creation's dawn as the Fa-ther speaks, the Son—who is the Word—carries out the creative work, and the Spirit fills the creation with heavenly presence: "In

---

[2] Frederick M. Lehman, "The Love of God," 1917.

the beginning, God created the heavens and the earth. The earth was without form and void, and darkness was over the face of the deep. And the Spirit of God was hovering over the face of the waters. And God said, 'Let there be light,' and there was light" (Gen. 1:1–3).

In *The Silmarillion*, J. R. R. Tolkien imagines the creation of the world as a divine chorale, with creation appearing out of nothingness like a glorious unfurling tapestry as God sings and the heavenly hosts watch in awe and wonder. It's easy to imagine it this way as you read the opening passages of Genesis. Each day builds momentum as the cast of creation makes its appearance.

First out of nothingness come the heaven and earth, then the explosion of light and the division of day and night. Once upon a time, there was no light. Then suddenly come billions of boiling stars and galaxies. The waters of the seas part and the Creator's imagination spins out majestic mountains and valleys, volcanos and rivers, deserts and icebergs, each one carved up by light and shadow. The song continues as life begins to teem and whir, grass takes root, and redwoods stretch heavenward. Kelp forests and grapevines sprawl and spin. Grasslands roll in rhythm with newborn tides.

Then come the animals. The dinosaurs. The dolphins. Lemmings and lightning bugs. Hummingbirds and wildebeests. There are themes like reptiles and bears, and variations upon each theme: polar bears, grizzly bears, black bears, Asiatic bears, panda bears. Creation has an improvisatory flair, bursting with imaginative energy and glory.

As God sings the song of creation, the creation responds with its own exaltations. "The heavens declare the glory of God," as the psalmist says (Ps. 19:1). Creation's song can be heard in the crash of perfect, spiraling waves on the coast of South Africa and the explosion of lava on Hawaii. Its melody is as subtle as the whirring of bees and as gentle as a breeze across the black hills of South Dakota. The psalmist isn't merely being metaphorical; he's noticing that God has imbued creation with a song that can be heard by ears tuned to the work of the Creator.

The Trinity's song roars to a climax on the sixth day. Dust is gathered and sculpted into flesh and bone, and into the new-formed lungs of Adam God gives man his first breath. Adam's first exhale is an entirely new kind of "hallelujah," the response of the firstborn image bearer of God.

Here, the Bible shows us that God isn't the disinterested god of the deists, who imagine him drawing up the world on a drafting board, winding it up like a clock, and leaving it to spin alone. Nor was creation a cosmic accident or the product of warring gods who sought to outdo one another.

Instead, the universe is the work of immeasurable brilliance, crafted with love and grace, and inhabited by the presence of the Creator, whose Word made the world and whose world sings of his glory, from the smallest blade of grass to the aurora borealis. Creation was made out of the overflow of God's own effusive and loving being, a reflection of the way the persons of the Trinity live in harmony, love, and community with one another.

And we were invited to join him in his song.

Adam: Creation's Worship Leader

Adam and Eve were the crown of creation, blessed with an image and breath given straight from the Creator, and tasked with carrying on the creative work on a scale suited to their smallness: subduing the earth and ruling over it (Gen. 1:28). God placed them in a garden called Eden, and the call to subdue the earth was an invitation to expand the garden out into the world around them. Adam and Eve were king and queen in a world ruled and inhabited by God, who reigned as King over them all.

The garden itself was more than an agricultural project.[3] It was a meeting place for God and man, where God "walked" among humanity (Gen. 3:8). It was the first temple, the first sacred space,

---

[3] For more on the garden of Eden as a temple, see G. K. Beale's excellent work *The Temple and the Church's Mission*, 68–80.

set apart from creation for the intersection of heaven and earth. Adam was, in a sense, the priest over all of creation, appointed by God to oversee it, steward it, and represent it before him.

But Adam wasn't leading worship services or doing ritualistic things to earn God's approval. There was no need; each moment of his life was a pleasing offering to God. Theologian John Witvliet defines worship as "the celebrative response to what God has done, is doing, and promises to do."[4] For Adam and Eve, all of life in Eden was an unbroken, loving response to God's work as their Creator, caretaker, and Lord. As they lived in harmony with him, it was as if they drew together all of creation's praise into a single and unified "hallelujah" and "amen." N. T. Wright summarizes this nicely when he says of creation, "We see a large, slowly developing story: of the good creator God making a wonderful world, and putting a Human in charge of it to rule it wisely and to gather up its grateful praise"[5]

This is how the universe is meant to work. God, in Trinity, creates the world. It's not part of him, but he nonetheless fills it with his presence and paints it with a vast panorama of beauty and brilliance, commissioning humankind to rule over it, nurture it, and enjoy it in his presence. Worship as an activity that's somehow separate from the rest of life appears nonexistent and, frankly, unnecessary. In the seamless perfection of that virgin world, it is all worship—a constant reflection of God's love, glory, and brilliance.

When we think about the story of worship with this as our point of origin, we see that worship starts with God. It begins in the loving relationships of the Trinity, where the Father exalts the Son, the Son exalts the Father, and the Spirit celebrates them both. This is what Harold Best calls "continuous outpouring."

> He cannot but give of himself, reveal himself, pour himself out. Even before he chooses to create, and before he chooses to reveal

---

[4] Witvliet, *Worship Seeking Understanding*, 31.
[5] Wright, *After You Believe*, 84.

himself beyond himself, he eternally pours himself out to his triune Self in unending fellowship, ceaseless conversation and immeasurable love unto an infinity of the same.[6]

Creation flows out of this glory-sharing outpouring, as the Three-in-One craft the universe together, imbuing it with beauty, mystery, and glory that is itself a reflection of the wonder and glory of God. Humanity is appointed the vanguard of creation, tasked with overseeing and subduing the earth, serving as priests of creation, and bearing God's image. Glory sharing flows between the members of the Trinity toward one another, and all of creation (including humanity) participates, responding to it and reflecting it through their perfect design and sinless life together. Humanity participates as glory bearers (Ps. 8:4–5) and glory beholders—living in wonder of our Creator and the glorious creation song that hums and buzzes around us.

All of this happens without a hint of ritual. There are no separated-out worship services; there is only the glorious and glorifying life lived with and unto God.[7] If someone were to ask Adam, "When do you worship God?" he might reply, "When do we not!" Worship isn't something other, external, compartmentalized, or confined. It is life with God, lived unto God for his glory and our pleasure.

Forgetting the Creator

Everything changes dramatically in Genesis 3, when the serpent creeps into the garden: "Did God actually say, 'You shall not eat of any tree in the garden'?" (Gen. 3:1).

Eve speaks up, saying, "We may eat of the fruit of the trees in the garden, but God said, 'You shall not eat of the fruit of the tree that is in the midst of the garden, neither shall you touch it, lest you die'" (Gen. 3:2–3). Eve defends God's integrity. The serpent,

---

[6] Best, *Unceasing Worship*, 21.
[7] See Boulton, *God against Religion*, 64: "In Genesis 2, the author . . . describes life in the garden in some detail, and yet we find in this description neither sanctuary nor altar, neither psalm nor sacrifice."

wanting to make God out to be oppressive, says in effect, "Does God not let you eat anything?" Eve affirms that God, indeed, let's them eat, but with one restriction; God has told them not to eat of the tree of knowledge.

> But the serpent said to the woman, "You will not surely die. For God knows that when you eat of it your eyes will be opened, and you will be like God, knowing good and evil." So when the woman saw that the tree was good for food, and that it was a delight to the eyes, and that the tree was to be desired to make one wise, she took of its fruit and ate, and she also gave some to her husband who was with her, and he ate. Then the eyes of both were opened, and they knew that they were naked. And they sewed fig leaves together and made themselves loincloths. (Gen. 3:4–7)

Up to this moment, nothing has ever been done apart from the life and love of God. Now, suddenly a whole new world opens up. The seed of that forbidden fruit will sprout deep in human hearts, spreading out roots and branches that will encompass the whole of humanity's future, blossoming into pride and envy, murder and deceit. Every crime, personal and corporate, private and public, grows out of this common root, from sex trafficking to genocide, adultery to petty theft. Life with God is rejected and life without God, embraced. The bite from that fruit is truly the kiss of death.

If worship is about "ascribing worth," then it's easy to see where worship goes wrong. Adam and Eve think what they'll gain from the fruit is of greater worth than what they have with God. They trust the serpent instead of God's promise. In Paul's words, they worship and serve created things—the serpent and themselves—rather than the Creator (Rom. 1:25).

In this new world apart from God, Adam and Eve are naked— their sinfulness is hopelessly exposed. They hurry to cover their shame with fig leaves, trying desperately to compensate for their new-felt vulnerability and exposure.

And they heard the sound of the LORD God walking in the garden in the cool of the day, and the man and his wife hid themselves from the presence of the LORD God among the trees of
the garden. But the LORD God called to the man and said to him,
"Where are you?" And he said, "I heard the sound of you in the
garden, and I was afraid, because I was naked, and I hid myself."
He said, "Who told you that you were naked? Have you eaten of
the tree of which I commanded you not to eat?" The man said,
"The woman whom you gave to be with me, she gave me fruit
of the tree, and I ate." Then the LORD God said to the woman,
"What is this that you have done?" The woman said, "The serpent deceived me, and I ate." (Gen. 3:8–13)

Adam and Eve can't even properly take responsibility for what
they've done. They cower in the trees until God calls them out.
Adam blames Eve ("the woman whom you gave to be with me")
and Eve blames the serpent ("the serpent deceived me").

The consequences are unavoidable, and God announces the
curses that they've brought upon themselves: Adam will suffer
and die, working ground that fights against him for the remain-
der of his days. Eve will suffer agony in childbirth and discord
in marriage. The serpent in particular faces the ultimate curse,
which for Adam and Eve is a promise: one of Eve's offspring will
crush his head.

Then comes a subtle and remarkable verse: "And the LORD
God made for Adam and for his wife garments of skins and
clothed them" (Gen. 3:21). Here, something wholly remarkable
happens. God seeks them out in their sin and shame, and then,
as Harold Best once put it, he "goes hunting for them."[8] Their
sin demands death, but God spares them by shedding the blood
of a proxy. An innocent creature is killed, and its flayed flesh is
made into a covering for Adam and Eve, a sign of both the cost
of their shame and the grace of their God, who spares their lives
and takes another. It's the first of many foreshadowings of the
cross in the Scriptures, a glimpse into the mysterious plan of

---

[8] From personal correspondence, April 2012.

God, written before the foundation of the world, to slay his Son in our place.

Into the Wilderness

Worship is essentially about ascribing worth. As sinless image bearers, Adam and Eve were part of creation's perpetual testimony to the worthiness—the goodness, glory, brilliance, and beauty—of God's handiwork. As soon as they sinned, they broke rank with that testimony, choosing to exalt and serve their own glory. They then faced the consequences of ascribing ultimate worth to themselves and were cast out of the lush comfort of the garden into the rocky soil of the wilderness. The abundant fruit that grew upon trees and vines was replaced with thorns and thistles. The sanctuary of the temple was replaced with the danger of the wild, with lurking beasts, vicious storms, and the greatest danger of all: the corrupted hearts of one another.

Genesis 1–3 is like a great Greek tragedy. They have it all and they fall so far, and yet God graciously pursues them. It's also a microcosm of everything the Bible has to tell us about worship.

Sin calls for death, and blood is shed in the garden, but not Adam's blood or Eve's. God himself takes the life of a substitute and wraps the naked frames of our great-grandparents in clothes that hide their shame. The broken worship they share with the serpent leaves them naked and humiliated, but before God sends them off into the barrens, he makes a sacrifice and a garb for them. It's a foretaste of worship restored, with Adam and Eve stepping again into participation with God's work as he stakes a bloody claim upon them and marks them as his own.

Chapter 2

WORSHIP IN THE
WILDERNESS

Life in the wilderness is a stark contrast to the comfort of the garden. In these barren lands, the harsh realities of life under the curse reveal themselves in both the darkness that consumes the hearts of mankind and the distance that becomes more evident between God and man.

What doesn't change is essential human nature. People are still made to bear God's image, still made to give and receive in the exchange of blessing and outpouring from God to creation and back again. As Harold Best describes it, we're continuously outpouring, perpetually worshiping something: "At this very moment, and for as long as this world endures, everybody inhabiting it is bowing down and serving something or someone—an artifact, a person, an institution, an idea, a spirit, or God through Christ."[1]

It's part of our hardwired, image-bearing heritage. Our lives are meant to inspire with (or inhale) the breath of God, the glory of his presence, the brilliance and beauty of his creation, and to expire (or exhale) an echo of wonder—an "amen." It should all be a single song, sung in harmony with the day-and-night heartbeat of creation.

But under the blinding pain of the curse, the song is shattered, and a thousand other songs begin to sound across the wilderness. Now, our outpouring is matched by an inner shame and desperation, and as we scan the stormy horizons outside of Eden, we look

---
[1]Best, *Unceasing Worship*, 17.

helplessly for a cure to our brokenness in the wilds that surround us. The beauty that was meant to inspire becomes the center of our hopes. The apostle Paul describes us: "They exchanged the truth about God for a lie and worshiped and served the creature rather than the Creator" (Rom. 1:25).

Just as Adam ceaselessly worshiped God in Eden, in the wild his worship continues unabated, but disconnected from the God who made him. Praise still pours forth, though missing its proper home.

Idols: Looking for Hope in the Wilderness

Idolatry is a word used quite a bit in the Scriptures, and it's a crucial part of the story of worship. The prophet Isaiah describes idolatry in its comic absurdity:

> The carpenter stretches a line; he marks it out with a pencil. He shapes it with planes and marks it with a compass. He shapes it into the figure of a man, with the beauty of a man, to dwell in a house. He cuts down cedars, or he chooses a cypress tree or an oak and lets it grow strong among the trees of the forest. He plants a cedar and the rain nourishes it. Then it becomes fuel for a man. He takes a part of it and warms himself; he kindles a fire and bakes bread. Also he makes a god and worships it; he makes it an idol and falls down before it. Half of it he burns in the fire. Over the half he eats meat; he roasts it and is satisfied. Also he warms himself and says, "Aha, I am warm, I have seen the fire!" And the rest of it he makes into a god, his idol, and falls down to it and worships it. He prays to it and says, "Deliver me, for you are my god!"
>
> They know not, nor do they discern, for he has shut their eyes, so that they cannot see, and their hearts, so that they cannot understand. No one considers, nor is there knowledge or discernment to say, "Half of it I burned in the fire; I also baked bread on its coals; I roasted meat and have eaten. And shall I make the rest of it an abomination? Shall I fall down before a block of wood?" He feeds on ashes; a deluded heart has led him astray, and he cannot deliver himself or say, "Is there not a lie in my right hand?" (Isa. 44:13–20)

This is the strange world of idolatry. While the carpenter clearly

is the master of the wood—growing the tree, cutting it down, carv-
ing and burning it—he misplaces his hope and bows down to worship the product of his hands. In doing so, he becomes like the
wood—blind, foolish, ignorant.

And yet, this picture is just pecking at the surface of what
idolatry means. Because of our constant outpouring, we're spilling
over with praise day and night, constantly testifying to the goodness and worth of something. Outside of Eden, outside of participation in the life of God, that outpouring is idolatry. We worship
self. We worship money. We worship power and sex. We worship
our spouses or children. We worship fantasies and myths.

In some ways, this is easy to see. Think of a political rally
where a crowd is whipped up into a frenzy, shouting cheers and
jeers as their political ideology is rehearsed, affirmed, and celebrated. Campaign speeches are loaded with promises that ring
of ultimate hopes—ending poverty, or bringing prosperity, peace,
strength, and dignity. The crowd helplessly erupts in agreement and affirmation, joining the worship leading of the stump
speech with their own heartfelt adoration of a politician or a
political ideal.

Worship isn't only something done consciously in songs,
prayers, and spiritual disciplines. Just as Adam's work in the garden celebrated and held up the glory of the Creator, his work
in the wilderness is an outpouring toward his ultimate hopes.
And so is yours and mine. The way we live our lives reveals our
idols. We religiously slave away at work, seeking affirmation from
achievement, status, and money. We pine night and day for love,
thinking that the right person would, as the cliché goes, "complete" us. We obsess over our children, thinking that our kids'
future success will provide the validation for which we hope.

Entertainment and Idolatry

Our entertainment industry knows how to aim for our idols. Whole
networks of programming are built around one or another idol.

The E! network holds out idols in the form of celebrities showing off fabulous lifestyles, walking red carpets, and partying in jet-set cities. We worship as we buy into the lie that they have it all—money, status, and happiness—our hearts swelling with desire when we see their Plasticine bodies and glittering wealth. "Deliver us," we think, as we imagine that if only we had what they have, we'd be happy.

We worship as we feel the pain of their divorces and drug addictions, weeping to see the temple of our idols in such a sad state of disarray. How could our gods of wealth and power disappoint us? How long will they be so far off?

Networks like ESPN offer twenty-four-hour worship of athleticism, sports teams, and with them, wealth, masculinity, and victory. Pornography is a temple of worship where the actors make a sacrifice of their bodies and dignity for money and fame, and the consumers make a sacrifice of their hearts, their marriages, and their cash for a god that titillates and pleases, if only for an instant.

The High Price of Idolatry

Most of these gods are fickle monsters, requiring greater risk, greater devotion, greater calluses upon eyes, hearts, and consciences as one progresses in their religion. Reality TV gets more scandalous and demeaning. Sports grow so competitive that performance-enhancing drugs and regulation-bending exchanges of money become normal and expected by both athlete and fan. Pornography becomes more violent, more demeaning, more destructive.

Worshipers, too, become transformed by their worship. As Isaiah says, they cannot see, they don't understand. They become image bearers of their gods—twisted and corrupted into something less than the glory for which they were created: the snarky cynicism of the perpetual culture critic; the obsessive fan who sweeps aside family and friends for games and championships; the porn addict who loses touch with anything close to a natural sexual identity.

Little could Adam and Eve know that such corruption would be birthed from their illicit meal in the garden, but this consequence isn't coincidental. There's a straight line between the stolen fruit and the broken lives of celebrities and addicts. In the aftermath of Eden, humanity is burdened with a deep sense of brokenness and vulnerability, and our entertainments and addictions all hold out the promise of deliverance. If only we were rich, if we were beautiful, if we were powerful, if we were high, if we were successful, if we were young, if we were victorious—if only, we think, we were relieved from the burden of shame that chased our parents into the wilderness.

So our worship pours out, looking for its rightful home, hoping that as we devote our lives to a cause or an ideal, to status or beauty, we will find a cure for the emptiness that rings so cavernously within us.

Religious Idolatry

Some, feeling that emptiness, turn to religion, hoping that in their high morals and obedience they can escape the grip of the curse. Here we can fool ourselves into thinking that we're rightly worshiping again. We approach God, thinking that the right actions, sacrifices, or beliefs would satisfy him and force him to welcome us back into the garden of his presence.

There are hints of this in the Bible's first story that's explicitly about worship, the story of Cain and Abel.

> Now Adam knew Eve his wife, and she conceived and bore Cain, saying, "I have gotten a man with the help of the LORD." And again, she bore his brother Abel. Now Abel was a keeper of sheep, and Cain a worker of the ground. In the course of time Cain brought to the LORD an offering of the fruit of the ground, and Abel also brought of the firstborn of his flock and of their fat portions. And the LORD had regard for Abel and his offering, but for Cain and his offering he had no regard. So Cain was very angry, and his face fell. The LORD said to Cain, "Why are you angry, and why has your face fallen? If you do well, will you not

be accepted? And if you do not do well, sin is crouching at the door. Its desire is for you, but you must rule over it."

Cain spoke to Abel his brother. And when they were in the field, Cain rose up against his brother Abel and killed him. (Gen. 4:1–8)

Here Cain and Abel are both worshipers. Their story falls on the heels of their parents' exile from Eden, and it tells us something profound about worship outside the garden's gates.

As a kid, I was told that Abel's offering was accepted because it included the blood of a sacrifice, and Cain's didn't, but that's not the real story. The passage offers clues showing us that the worshipers' hearts were what differentiated between them.

Cain's sacrifice is presented in the text without much information. "Cain brought to the Lord an offering of the fruit of the ground." Theologian Bruce Waltke[2] points out that the word used for "offering" here is used elsewhere in the Hebrew Bible for grain offerings, which means that blood wasn't the issue.

Instead, the contrast between the two offerings comes from everything else we know about Abel's offering. He brings the "firstborn of his flock" and "their fat portions." These are anything but superfluous details. Abel's offering acknowledges the lordship of God over creation. It flows from a heart that knows its place, its smallness in the scope of creation. Giving the firstborn says to God that he comes first, and giving the fat portions says that he deserves the best. Abel is acknowledging that all of life is a gift, flowing from God's generous, creative grace. His offering is a response to that provision.

Cain, by contrast, is just showing up. He knows he needs to make an offering, but it's an offering of mere obligation, not of love or humility. God is given neither the first nor the best, and this reeks of Genesis 3. Forgetting who God is and what he's done, Cain reserves the best for himself, ignoring that all he has comes as a gift. He makes an offering, and he expects God to reciprocate this offering with acceptance. Just as his parents stole something

---

[2] Waltke, "Cain and His Offering," 366.

and were rejected, Cain offers something and wants to be accepted again.[3]

It's a simple exchange—obey and be accepted—but Cain's attempt to undo the work of the curse fails to see how deep and wide the rift is between God and man. Abel's offering is made in faith, acknowledging the God who created all and promised redemption to Eve, but Cain's offering, made out of rote obligation and with a hollow heart that believes "God owes me," is rejected.

This sends Cain into a rage, and history's first dispute over worship results in a cold-blooded murder.

> Then the LORD said to Cain, "Where is Abel your brother?" He said, "I do not know; am I my brother's keeper?" And the LORD said, "What have you done? The voice of your brother's blood is crying to me from the ground. And now you are cursed from the ground, which has opened its mouth to receive your brother's blood from your hand. When you work the ground, it shall no longer yield to you its strength. You shall be a fugitive and a wanderer on the earth." Cain said to the LORD, "My punishment is greater than I can bear. Behold, you have driven me today away from the ground, and from your face I shall be hidden. I shall be a fugitive and a wanderer on the earth, and whoever finds me will kill me." Then the LORD said to him, "Not so! If anyone kills Cain, vengeance shall be taken on him sevenfold." And the LORD put a mark on Cain, lest any who found him should attack him. Then Cain went away from the presence of the LORD and settled in the land of Nod, east of Eden. (Gen. 4:9–16)

Here, then, is the first of history's many worship wars, where the children of Adam and Eve will literally draw blood over their disputes about how to worship God.

Once again we see God's grace: instead of executing Cain for his crime, God spares his life. Though he sends him further into exile and destines him to wander in the wilderness, he also marks him, just as he marked Adam and Eve with their animal-skin coverings. Cain's exile is both a mark of shame, exposing him as a

---

[3] Boulton, *God against Religion*, 85.

murderer and villain, and a mark of grace,[4] with God saying, "He belongs to me, and I will protect him."

God isn't done with Cain because he isn't done with any of us. Ultimately, the future hope of worship rests not on the shoulders of any of us getting the equation right, but on the God who promises to restore it.

Worship in the wilderness pours forth from Adam and all of his line of descendants: from Cain and from all of us. We live toward hopes, dreams, and desires, and apart from our Creator, we're willing to "feed upon ashes" (Isa. 44:20) because we're so blind and so desperate for something that can satisfy our empty hearts.

History is full of noisy eruptions of praise, cacophonous announcements of the answer to that desperation. They rang in the jackbooted marches through Nuremberg, and they erupt in the toasts and cheers of corporate boardrooms. They appear in the climax of a thousand films as love triumphs or good defeats evil. They resound in coliseums and stadiums, as crowds roar over victories or sing along to an international supergroup. Our lives and efforts are a constant eruption of praise for this hope or that one, each rooted in a longing for redemption.

And they all disappoint. No matter their volume, no matter their strength, the hopes held forth by the songs of the wilderness perpetually fall short of being a real cure.

Even so, another song continues. It's remarkably faint and easy to miss, like the rustling of earth as a mustard seed sprouts and breaks the surface of the ground. It's an old, old song—perhaps the oldest, birthed in an age before the first day, a dream hatched in the heart of the Trinity before light dawned on the new creation. It's a song God is singing and a song he'll continue to sing as the children of Eve wander and look for hope.

Soon, in the midst of the wandering hearts of men, God begins to whisper the next verse.

---

[4] Plantinga, "A Mark of Grace" (sermon).

Chapter 3

THE SONG OF ISRAEL

The years go by, and the law of entropy takes its toll on the wilderness. The order and harmony of creation give way to the more chaotic, a world tangled in bramble and thistle. There is more murder. More evil. More shadow ruling the broken hearts of men. The madness reaches such a pitch that the Lord searches the earth for one righteous man. With him, God will wash the face of the earth clean and begin again.

After forty days and forty nights of worldwide floods, the earth is wiped clean, and when the water recedes, Noah and his family descend from their gopher-wood shelter onto the still-damp ground. One would think that in the aftermath of such widespread judgment, Noah would be on his best behavior, but the old man can't stay away from the booze, he gets drunk, and the curse shows how hard-fought its removal will be.

Nonetheless, it's all part of the story that God is telling. And into the story wanders Abram. There's not much to say about Abram before God shows up. We know he was a semi-nomadic herdsman. Many believe he was a pagan—a star worshiper, to be precise. We know he was old, and we know that by all appearances, he and his wife were sterile. The story that unfolds shows him to be quick to lose heart, willing to prostitute his wife, and all too eager to jump into bed with one of his slave girls, eventually abandoning her and the son he fathered through her.

Yet this is the man God chooses to use for the next phase of his plan. Through Abram, he will begin to teach this lost and broken world a new song.

The Promise

God tells him, "Fear not, Abram, I am your shield; your reward will be very great" (Gen. 15:1).

Childless, landless, and very old, Abram isn't so sure. "O Lord God, what will you give me, for I continue childless, and the heir of my house is Eliezer of Damascus? . . . Behold, you have given me no offspring, and a member of my household will be my heir" (Gen. 15:2–3).

In the face of Abram's challenge, God gives him a promise and makes him a guarantee. First the promise: "This man shall not be your heir; your very own son shall be your heir." Then God brings Abram outside and says, "Look toward heaven, and number the stars, if you are able to number them." And he adds, "So shall your offspring be" (Gen. 15:4–5).

Under that glittering panorama, God promises Abram innumerable heirs. He not only makes the promise; he follows it with the assurance that it will be kept.

> "Bring me a heifer three years old, a female goat three years old, a ram three years old, a turtledove, and a young pigeon." And he brought him all these, cut them in half, and laid each half over against the other. But he did not cut the birds in half. And when birds of prey came down on the carcasses, Abram drove them away.
>
> . . . When the sun had gone down and it was dark, behold, a smoking fire pot and a flaming torch passed between these pieces. On that day the Lord made a covenant with Abram, saying, "To your offspring I give this land, from the river of Egypt to the great river, the river Euphrates, the land of the Kenites, the Kenizzites, the Kadmonites, the Hittites, the Perizzites, the Rephaim, the Amorites, the Canaanites, the Girgashites and the Jebusites." (Gen. 15:9–11, 17–21)

To our modern imaginations, this seems violent and primitive. For Abram, this was a clear and plain statement, simple as signing a contract. It would have been standard practice for Abram and his neighbors to do a similar ceremony whenever they wanted to make a deal: split an animal, stand in the midst of its shed blood and broken carcass, and make an oath. Symbolically, the sacrifice would remind both parties of the weight of their oath. Should the covenant be broken by one of the members, such violence should be expected in retribution.[1]

Here with Abram, God enters into just such a promise, saying in essence: "I will bless you. You will father a child. You will have this land." But strangely, it's a one-sided promise. Abram doesn't stand in the midst of the carcasses. He makes no vow. He merely watches and believes as the torch and smoking firepot pass between them, and he is the recipient of God's promise.

Once again, God is making a profound statement. What he starts, he'll finish. What he promises, he'll do, with or without any particular aid from us. God thereby inaugurates a new phase in his plan, wherein his promise to Eve extends particularly to Abram—renamed Abraham—and his offspring.

A Strange Family Tree

Eventually the promised child is born: Isaac, whose name means "laughter," the child inconceivably conceived by an elderly mother who could only laugh at the thought of having a baby. He too becomes the bearer of the promise. Then his son Jacob, a swindler and a cheat, wrestles with God and walks away with a limp and the mantle of the promise.

They are a family of lushes and adulterers, liars and lunatics, chasing voices in the wilderness, waging war and risking all for this promise whispered under the stars. When we hear the word *patriarch* or the majestic phrase "the God of Abraham, Isaac, and Jacob," we tend to imagine stalwart, bearded saints, whose character and faithfulness make them worthy of mention. But in fact, they are broken ne'er-do-wells whose significance goes to highlight that God is the one who remains faithful through thick

---

[1] Hamilton, *The Book of Genesis*, 430.

and thin. He makes and keeps his promises, and our forefathers believe through tears and darkness.

The song of the patriarchs is a song born of weeping, of too much drink, of long suffering, of hopeless sojourns and agonizing compromise. It's not a song of affluence and triumph. It's not the song of the saintly, sung in white robes and accompanied by choirs of angels and pitch-perfect orchestration. It sounds far more like drunken sailors, wailing a hazy lament in a land far from home, who look to the stars and feel the haunting presence of the promise, clinging to that twilit hope in spite of their circumstances, in spite of the curse, in spite of themselves. God is going to keep his word. They weep for it. They gnash their teeth over it. One even gets into a brawl with God and demands it.

The Exodus

The passing of years doesn't breed much hope. There is famine and slavery. After four hundred years under the thumb of Pharaoh, the children of Abraham are now a nation, but a nation enslaved by a cruel tyrant. Rumors of an overthrow begin to spread—a redeemer will lead them out of chains—and Pharaoh lashes out, killing the firstborn sons of an entire generation. Israel's mothers weep; the promise seems dimmer than ever.

Pharaoh's daughter finds a baby in a river, a child floating in a basket of bulrushes hidden among the sedge and reeds. She pulls him out of the water, names him Moses, and raises him as her own. He rises to great heights in Pharaoh's government until he commits murder and is exiled, sent like so many before him out of the familiar and into the wilderness. There he meets the fiery presence of the Creator, who has yet to abandon his plans for the children of Abraham and who intends to make a statement that will cause all Egypt to tremble at the mention of his name.

We've probably all seen this movie. Hopefully you've read the story before. Moses returns from exile and demands that Pharaoh let his people go. Nine times he asks; nine times he's denied. And with each denial, God unleashes a plague upon the Egyptians, each plague a declaration of war on the gods of Egypt. The Egyptians worshiped the Nile as the lifeblood of their empire, and the God of Moses turns it to blood. The Egyptians worshiped a frog-god and the God of Moses shows that he rules over the frogs, sending them raining down from heaven. Then come gnats, flies, massive death of livestock, boils, hail, locusts, and then the blotting out of the sun. Even Ra, the Egyptian sun-god who was believed to rule over the whole universe, is no match for the power of the God of Moses.

And yet Pharaoh refuses to relinquish his grip on the slave nation.

Finally comes the worst plague of all: the death of the firstborn. God's wrath has been awakened by the hard-heartedness of Pharaoh, and now the God of Israel will show the fiercest display of wrath since the great flood. All of Egypt's firstborn—from the king's to the slaves' to the livestock—all will be killed. But Pharaoh's heart is hardened. He doesn't listen.

Moses gathers the people of Israel together to warn of what is coming.

> Then Moses called all the elders of Israel and said to them, "Go and select lambs for yourselves according to your clans, and kill the Passover lamb. Take a bunch of hyssop and dip it in the blood that is in the basin, and touch the lintel and the two doorposts with the blood that is in the basin. None of you shall go out of the door of his house until the morning. For the LORD will pass through to strike the Egyptians, and when he sees the blood on the lintel and on the two doorposts, the LORD will pass over the door and will not allow the destroyer to enter your houses to strike you. You shall observe this rite as a statute for you and for your sons forever. And when you come to the land that the LORD will give you, as he has promised, you shall keep this service. And when your children say to you, 'What do you mean by this service?' you shall say, 'It is the sacrifice of the LORD's Passover, for he passed over the houses of the people of Israel in Egypt,

when he struck the Egyptians but spared our houses.'" And the people bowed their heads and worshiped.

Then the people of Israel went and did so; as the LORD had commanded Moses and Aaron, so they did.

At midnight the LORD struck down all the firstborn in the land of Egypt, from the firstborn of Pharaoh who sat on his throne to the firstborn of the captive who was in the dungeon, and all the firstborn of the livestock. (Ex. 12:21–29)

Only after this does the king relent, and Israel leaves their chains behind as Egypt weeps. Not long after, the king's anger is reawakened. He's lost his firstborn, his gods have been humiliated, and his people weep bitterly. Meanwhile, this slave nation—the source of his turmoil—walks away unscathed. The loss of livestock and slaves is a bitter economic blow, and the victory of God over the king is a crushing blow to his pride and power. Suddenly he rises, determined to have revenge and return Israel to their chains.

Armed to the teeth, Pharaoh and his armies descend on the caravan. The people turn on Moses, crying out, "Is it because there are no graves in Egypt that you have taken us away to die in the wilderness? What have you done to us in bringing us out of Egypt?" (Ex. 14:11). Moses, in turn, cries out to God, the sea parts, and the people of Israel pass safely through a watery grave. When the Egyptian armies attempt to pass, the watery walls collapse and all of Pharaoh's army is drowned.

The God of Israel is a God who shows up, shows his power over the other Gods, crushes his enemies, and rescues his people. He isn't far off. He's right in front of them, day and night, in a billowing cloud of smoke and steam and a bright burning column of fire. This God dwells with his people.

Israel's journey through the desert and toward the land God promised to Abraham is tumultuous as they wrestle with faith and doubt, victory and defeat. In the midst of it, God reveals further what it means for him is to dwell with his people: an elaborate system of sacrifices, priests, tabernacles, and holy places.

Israel's Worship: Bleeding Birds and Bleeding Beasts

It is here, friends, that I feel the need to hit the brakes on the story and have a bit of a face-to-face conversation. I'll start with a confession: I used to think this stuff didn't matter. Not because it didn't matter in *history*. Not because it didn't matter in *theology*. I thought it didn't matter because it didn't matter to *me*. And the odds are high that if you're honest, you'd say the same thing.

We are children of a much more sanitized era, you and I. Most of us have never taken the life of an animal larger than a trout, and even if we have, it's probably been an event of such novelty as to be utterly disconnected from ordinary living. The carnivores among us buy our meat well butchered and shrink-wrapped, and the vegetarians among us probably feel an even greater disdain for the culture of animal sacrifice and bloodshed in the Old Testament.

So when we engage with the story of the Old Testament, the Passover, and the temple, we have a certain sense of disregard or distance for the bloody practices that punctuate Israel's rhythms of life. If we're entirely honest, we probably find the whole thing a bit gross.

Thankfully, we think, we've been shielded from such gore. The sentiment of most contemporary Christian worship is high on emotional language, heavy on the Spirit (and its accompanying imagery of flames, wind, and doves), but usually thin on (if not bereft of) the topic of bleeding birds and beasts.[2] We talk about the cross as shorthand for the bloody sacrifice of Jesus, but even that is removed from the hands-on messiness of Israel's worship.

But any conversation about the story of worship forces us to detour into the viscera of animal sacrifice. Reading through Exodus and Leviticus can feel like a trip through an ancient butcher shop, with rules about the age and purity of livestock, ritualistic practices for killing them and draining their blood, and regulations for burning their flesh. Like a trip to a foreign land, it all requires getting familiar with some of the local dialect: clean and

---

[2] This phrase comes from Isaac Watts's hymn version of Psalm 51.

unclean, arks and covenants, tabernacles and holy places, and of course, the Holy of Holies or Most Holy Place. If we're not careful, it can start to sound like Dungeons and Dragons.

Add to that the pop culture view of this strange world, best exemplified by *Raiders of the Lost Ark* and the melting faces of the Nazis in the blaze of the opened ark. Altogether, it's a difficult pill to swallow—a mysterious and violent time and place. No wonder we write it off, preferring to think of it all as metaphor and imagery, rather than a very real, earthy reality in which God lived in community with mankind.

But as Christians, we don't get a pass on this part of the story. The story of God and Israel is the story of God and us. The bleary hope sung by the patriarchs became a tearful slave song in Egypt, and in the deserts on the other side of the Red Sea another movement of the song began. "God lives with Israel" was the title of the movement. Its rhythms were carved into the flesh of lambs and goats, punctuated by a river of blood flowing out of the temple and shouts of "glory, hallelujah" as the divine presence filled the tabernacle.

Worship and Sinai

To pick up the story, then, this national caravan of freed slaves wanders on through a desert wasteland, feeding on bread from heaven and warding off enemies until they find themselves at the foot of a mountain called Sinai. There Moses retreats to the top of the mountain to converse with God about their future.

For the rest of the book of Exodus, God lays out the framework for his relationship with Israel.

> You yourselves have seen what I did to the Egyptians, and how I bore you on eagles' wings and brought you to myself. Now therefore, if you will indeed obey my voice and keep my covenant, you shall be my treasured possession among all peoples, for all the earth is mine; and you shall be to me a kingdom of priests and a holy nation. These are the words that you shall speak to the people of Israel. (Ex. 19:4–6)

Theologian Marva Dawn has pointed out that the introduction of the law begins with grace.[3] God intervenes and redeems first, then calls his people to respond to their rescue by living the new identity he's given them. As if to say, "You were once slaves, but I rescued you and defeated your captors, and I'm now calling you to be a kingdom of priests," God reveals himself and invites Israel to be his special people.

Notice as well that God's mission isn't merely to establish a holy huddle with Israel, but is also through Israel to bless the whole world. It's a throwback to the garden with a similar mandate—be fruitful and multiply, be priests to the nations. Adam was to have given birth to a kingdom of priests, ruling over and subduing the whole earth, joining up creation's declarations of praise into a unified song to the Creator. Israel has the same charge. They are to be a beacon of worship in the wilderness, a voice of protest to the idolatry of the nations.

And so begins the revelation of the law. For much of what follows, God defines the terms of their relationship, but it's all prefaced by the Passover and the exodus; all of God's demands come in the light of what God has done to rescue Israel. He will live in their midst, and they will truly be a beacon to the world because of it.

In the years that follow, as Israel struggles to keep the law, God continues to call them back to himself and continues to roll out his plan. What he gives them at Sinai is a system of sacrifices—a process by which they can approach his presence, and he can remain among them. Through it, worship is restored (in part) to Israel. For the purposes of our story, we'll look at three aspects that defined Israel's relationship with God.

The Temple

In Exodus 25, God begins giving instructions on the construction of his dwelling place—the tabernacle. Generations later, King David will build a temple to house this dwelling place, but the

---

[3] Dawn, "But It" (sermon).

purpose is essentially the same: God will have a house of his own in the middle of the ordinary lives of his people.

It is a house built for a king. God tells Moses to take a collection from the people—not out of obligation, notice, but "from every man whose heart moves him" (Ex. 25:2). God wants the gifts to flow from cheerful, responsive hearts of worship (see also 2 Cor. 9:7). They collect rare metals, fabrics, wood, fur, and jewels to make the temple a hub of wealth and glory.

The instructions start with the ark of the covenant, in which the law is to be kept and upon which God's presence will be manifest. There is an outer tent and an inner tent, and ultimately, the Holy of Holies—the place where the presence of God is particularly and uniquely present.

While many world religions worship gods in temples, Israel's claim was unique. Theirs wasn't simply a consecrated center for worship; it was a meeting place where the Lord of the creation actually met face-to-face with humans. G. K. Beale points out that much of the language that describes the temple echoes descriptions of life in the garden.[4] The continuity is no accident: these two places serve the same purpose.

The garden was meant to be the hub of worship, a meeting place wherein the goodness of creation was gathered up and offered to God in the perfect lives of Adam and Eve. Outside the garden was the wilderness, an unkempt place that Adam and his children would ultimately subdue and fill, incorporating it all in the worshiping life of Eden.

The temple is a redemptive step toward restoring all that was lost when Adam and Eve fell. Here, God will meet again with his people (under profoundly different conditions), and they'll serve as a beacon to the nations, a ringing invitation for the broken world to return to worshiping its Maker. Rather than subduing and filling the uninhabited wilderness of a perfect world, Israel is charged with subduing the populated wilderness of a fallen world, where

---

[4] Beale, *The Temple and the Church's Mission*, 66–80.

Satan and the sons of men collude in a project of death and decay. Through Israel, God means to turn back that project and shine light into the darkness of the world, and that light's bright epicenter is the temple.

But it's profoundly unsafe for us if God simply shows up. His presence is "terrible" to sinners (to borrow an older use of the word).[5] Terror has a strong grip upon our imaginations, and most of us would probably prefer to leave it disassociated from the loving, comforting God we've come to expect. A terrible God is anathema to us because we've lost sight of the God of Israel, who we're told in Scripture is a consuming fire. His descent onto Mount Sinai to reveal the law to Moses was life-threatening to the bystanders.

> On the morning of the third day there were thunders and lightnings and a thick cloud on the mountain and a very loud trumpet blast, so that all the people in the camp trembled. . . . Now Mount Sinai was wrapped in smoke because the LORD had descended on it in fire. The smoke of it went up like the smoke of a kiln, and the whole mountain trembled greatly. . . .
>
> And the LORD said to Moses, "Go down and warn the people, lest they break through to the LORD to look and many of them perish." (Ex. 19:16, 18, 21)

Fire, smoke, thunder, and death accompany the presence of God. This is the price of sin for a fallen world, where once God could dwell in glory and we could dwell in safety. Now his holiness blazes in our sin-stained atmosphere, a scorching warning to those who would dare go near him apart from some measure of protection.

"Build me a temple," he tells Moses in effect, "a dwelling place where I can safely be among you." It's not an ego statement—give me all your gold and wealth. It's not merely ritual, and it's not

---

[5] Isaac Watts has a hymn with this opening stanza:

Terrible God, that reign'st on high,
How awful is thy thundering hand!
Thy fiery bolts how fierce they fly!
Nor can all earth or hell withstand.

simply about institutionalizing the religion. Instead, the temple itself is a means of God's immense grace. By inhabiting a temple behind layers of curtains, high walls, and levels of protection, God shields his people from the unbearable, fiery reaction of sin's exposure to holiness.

The Priest

Even after the temple is established, not just anyone can march behind the curtains. One can almost imagine a cluster of Israel's men, standing outside the temple while it boils with light and smoke, looking fearfully at one another saying, "You go in there."

"No way, dude. You first."

Fortunately, God makes plans that eliminate this debate in Exodus 28–29, inaugurating the priesthood with Aaron and his sons. These men will be the mediators between God and men, a set-apart class of religious men who care for the temple and carry out the religious work of making offerings on behalf of the people. Israel will gather at the temple, and the priests will facilitate their worship, making the sacrifices, passing through the curtains and standing before God's presence, and returning to the people to offer assurance that God has heard their prayers and forgiven their sins.

Just as Adam stood as the chief representative of creation before God, the priests represent God's people, and their work gathers up Israel's praise in one voice, offering it in an acceptable way—which brings us to the third element: the sacrifices.

The Sacrifices

The climax of Israel's worship was the sacrifice, and there were many of them. There were sacrifices for the dedication of the priests. There were sacrifices for the dedication of the temple. There were ordinary, everyday sacrifices and sacrifices for big, once-a-year celebrations. There were sacrifices for the priests and sacrifices for the poor. There were sacrifices for the sick, for the healed, and for childbirth. Worship in Israel was a bloody, costly thing. Wealth in those days was measured in flocks and fields, and the demands of Israel's God were expensive.

It was very clear that apart from such sacrifices, there was no way the arrangement could continue. God is holy, and Israel was not. They needed to shed blood for sins both great and small so that God could dwell in their midst. Sin demands death, and Israel couldn't live in community with God without a clear, violent, and ever-present reminder of the cost of their sins.

Through all of these steps, the God of Israel extended the invitation to the children of Abraham, essentially saying: "I am your God, I rescued you from the chains of your bondage. Now I want to live among you, standing you up as a beacon for the world, a testimony to life as it was meant to be lived."

Life with God in Israel

While we might be frightened by the blood and gore, let's not forget this crucial point: this was the best thing going. There was no better way of worship in the world. God dwelled with Israel, and with no one else.

Let's also remember that this was all evidence of God's grace. Nothing *required* God to provide a way for redeeming fallen man. He had every right to simply allow us to suffer the deadly consequences of our actions, but he didn't. He never abandoned us. He stepped into our world and made a way for us to know him.

It's beautiful to see how King David, in the throes of guilt and repentance, acknowledges that this whole system is God's way of providing for us. Though the actions of Israel's praise are all carried out by human hands and mediators, David, in his great prayer of confession in Psalm 51, nonetheless cries out to God, "Purge me with hyssop" (v. 7). He doesn't cry out to the priest. He knows that God must be the one to wash him clean.

David can cry out to God this way because he knows that worship in Israel, like worship in Eden, is always and only participation in God's own glorious and glory-sharing life. Moreover, after the fall, true worship is always participation in God's redemptive work. It's not a mechanical exchange where, if we get the details right, God is required to forgive us. Rather, it's a heart-touched reality wherein God promises to redeem, and Israel, in faithful, believing response to those promises, participated in that redemptive work through the sacrificial system.

Worship, Wrath, and Holiness

There's a tendency to view the God of Israel as somehow different from the God of the New Testament. The common misconception is that God was more wrathful and angry in the Old Testament, more harsh in his treatment of Israel and her enemies, than he is in the New Testament. After all, there are some fearsome stories about this God's wrath—many of which center on Israel's worship practices. In Leviticus 10, two of Aaron's sons enter the temple and worship with "unauthorized fire" (or "strange fire," as the King James Version puts it). This means that they are breaking the rules that God gave Moses for how they are to worship him.

Things go poorly for them.

> Now Nadab and Abihu, the sons of Aaron, each took his censer and put fire in it and laid incense on it and offered unauthorized fire before the LORD, which he had not commanded them. And fire came out from before the LORD and consumed them, and they died before the LORD. Then Moses said to Aaron, "This is what the LORD has said: 'Among those who are near me I will be sanctified, and before all the people I will be glorified.'" And Aaron held his peace. (Lev. 10:1–3)

God strikes them dead for worshiping him in a way he hasn't prescribed.

Similarly, in 2 Samuel 6:5–7, we read the story of Uzzah. Uzzah is overseeing the return of the ark of the covenant to Israel after it was captured by enemies. The Israelites are bringing it home on an ox cart (which is itself a violation of how God commanded them to transport it) and Uzzah is anxious to see it home safe. As they're traveling, one of the oxen stumbles, and Uzzah reaches out his hand to steady the ark, fearful of letting this sacred object tumble off the cart and into the roadside filth. God strikes him dead as soon as he touches the ark.

These are only two examples of death from the hands of God, and there are many more. It's stories like these that make people think there must be something different about the Old Testament God and the New Testament God. The God Jesus speaks of surely wouldn't be so arbitrary, so harsh, they reason. Perhaps they were two different Gods, or perhaps Jesus changed the nature of God by becoming human. Perhaps God was just more compassionate after the incarnation, more sympathetic, less angry.

But this perspective underestimates two crucial facts: the holiness of God and the sinfulness of fallen man. The boiling, fiery, deadly presence of God is the *natural reaction* of holiness in the presence of sin. Our God is likened to a refining fire—a raging inferno that burns away impurity and leaves only what is purified and perfect (Mal. 3:2–3). We misunderstand the wrath of God if we think it's only emotional rage, like an angry, frustrated parent. It's not; it's a rage made of a pure, perfect, and holy hatred of sin and evil. On the flip side, it's a rage built upon the deepest love of what is good, pure, and perfect. Such wisdom and love can only respond with disgust at evil's destructive grip on the good.

Just as we underestimate God's holiness, we underestimate how deeply sinful we are. We think of ourselves as good enough, smart enough, and likeable enough to *deserve* forgiveness from God. Shouldn't God overlook minor offenses from people like Aaron's sons or Uzzah? Aren't their hearts in the right place? Shouldn't poor Uzzah—anxious to see God's ark protected from the filth—be shown some grace when he sets out his hand to stabilize it?

But Uzzah's sin is much like ours. He fails to see how holy and pure God is, and how deeply sinful and impure he himself is. As

R. C. Sproul once said, "Uzzah presumed his hands were cleaner than the dirt. God said no."[6]

Israel's Invitation

God says it again and again: outside of Eden we can't bear his presence. True holiness in the presence of sinfulness results in a deadly reaction, like fire and gasoline or potassium and water (Google it).

And yet, Israel is given an invitation and a way into God's presence. If we truly understand how holy God is, we'll see that all of the actions of the temple were evidence of grace. The walls of the temple weren't about protecting the holy places from the people, but about protecting the people from the overwhelming holiness of God. The priesthood was established not as ranks of exclusivity— as if God were trying to keep us away from him—but as the best means for providing some kind of access to him. And the sacrifices weren't the demands of an egotistical tyrant but the necessary demands of sin, horrifying evidence of how far we've fallen from the love-filled community of Eden. They were God's way of redeeming people from a world so sin-sick that his presence in our midst resulted in earthquakes and storms of billowing smoke and flame.

The Song of Israel

Sadly, this arrangement is perpetually interrupted in the history of Israel. Throughout the years, they're seen stumbling, failing, falling away to worship the gods of their neighbors, forgetting the One who called them out of Egypt.

Even so, God keeps seeking, inviting, and calling to them. The Old Testament is the story of God rescuing Israel and calling them back to repentance again and again. They fail to keep their promises over and over, but God continually shows up, calls them back, and provides a way for them to be forgiven, keeping the promise he made to Abraham in the midst of the broken bodies and shed blood of the sacrifices.

---

[6] Sproul, "Holiness and Justice" (sermon).

This is the song of Israel. It begins with the starlit hope of the patriarchs as they sing bleary-eyed songs of their promised future. It becomes a slave song, sung in the chains of Egypt, and evolves into the road song of a tribe in the desert. Once they settle into the Promised Land, it becomes a declaration: "God lives in Israel!" It's a violent song, written with fire and bloodstains, and it's a song of failure and reconciliation.

Most of all, it's a song written by God himself. The promise made to Abraham was kept not by Abraham and not by his children, but by the God who said, "Let me be cursed before I break this vow."[7] The promise was the hope of the world, the one place where God himself dwelled with man, an echo of Eden, and a foretaste of a future too good to imagine.

---

[7] Hamilton, *The Book of Genesis*, 430.

Chapter 4

THE SONG OF JESUS

As the years roll by, two realities continue to reassert themselves in the life and worship of Israel. First, there is Israel's perpetual infidelity. Discontent with the kingship of God, they demand a human king like all their neighbors and enemies. God gives them their wish, and Saul, first appearing as the golden boy of the struggling state, shows the problem with human kings—tyrannical rule. This gives way to David, who is yet another promising figure of integrity and faith, but whose adultery leads to murder and public disgrace. And so goes the line of Israel's kings.

They build a glorious temple, a declaration to the world that here in Israel and in Israel alone is the Maker of heaven and earth. Pilgrims make their way to Jerusalem from all over the kingdom to worship on the Day of Atonement, when a river of blood pours from the temple, and the presence of God fills it with glory. And still they forget their God.

As Israel's failures mount up, voices begin calling from the desert, rumors from fiery vagabonds in the wasteland, hinting at a chosen One, a suffering servant who will carry our guilt on his shoulders, whose body will be a gateway through which the Spirit of God makes his way into men's hearts both great and small. These rumors pile up, a simmering rumble of hope even as Israel's failures lead to their ultimate disgrace: the destruction of the temple and the displacement of their people.

Though they eventually return from exile, things are never the same. They watch and wait, eagerly anticipating this promised One who will restore their marred glory and stabilize their broken world.

Years go by. Tyrants remain. Hopes dim. And then, a young Jewish girl starts to sing a new song:

My soul magnifies the Lord,
    and my spirit rejoices in God my Savior,
for he has looked on the humble estate of his servant.
    For behold, from now on all generations will call me
        blessed;
for he who is mighty has done great things for me,
    and holy is his name.
And his mercy is for those who fear him
    from generation to generation.
He has shown strength with his arm;
    he has scattered the proud in the thoughts of their hearts;
he has brought down the mighty from their thrones
    and exalted those of humble estate;
he has filled the hungry with good things,
    and the rich he has sent away empty.
He has helped his servant Israel,
    in remembrance of his mercy,
as he spoke to our fathers,
    to Abraham and to his offspring forever. (Luke 1:46–55)

Young Mary is about to bear a child whose name will be Jesus, and he will be the one through whom the world is made new. Her song from Luke 1 shows us that she knows this is the promised One, a suffering servant and a warrior King, one Reggie Kidd calls the "Singing Savior,"[1] born not only as Mary's child, but by the power of the Holy Spirit. He is God in flesh.

The Irony of the Gospel

The incarnation isn't merely a doctrinal fact (though it certainly is that) or a footnote in this story; it's powerful and ironic poetry affirming the faithfulness of God. Though creation's first daughter failed to remember her God, her God never fails to remember her. He made a promise to her, and as the history unfolds, he brings

---

[1] Kidd uses this phrase throughout his excellent book *With One Voice*, which looks at how all of Christian worship is participation in the worship of the Father as led by the Son.

about its most pivotal event through the virginal womb of one of her daughters. Mary, like the generations of patriarchs and kings before her, is drawn by God into participation in the grand narrative of redemption. The wonder of her pregnancy is a testimony not to her own perfections, but to the God who keeps his promise.

This sense of holy irony runs throughout the story of Jesus. He is the king of the universe, born into barnyard filth, living in obscurity for most of his life. The Lord of the Sabbath breaks the Sabbath laws. God enfleshed spends his time not with the purified elites in the temple, but among the godless and unclean: sex workers, thugs, sailors, cripples, and lepers.

By this time, Israel is under the rule of Rome, dreaming of a time when they can drive the Romans out and relive the glory days of their former kingdom. When their promised King shows up, he marches like a lamb to the slaughter, uninterested in political and geographic turf wars. To those around him, he seems like a failure. If he is God's Son, can't he defeat the Romans? Can't he restore Israel's glory as God's dwelling place? Can't he build a kingdom that dominates the whole world?

The answer is, "of course he can." But it would be a near-meaningless victory in a much larger, much more horrific battle. You see, the difference between Jesus and Israel is that Jesus has never forgotten God's word. He has never forgotten the promise. He was there when God said to Eve, "he will strike his heel," and he knows that bearing Satan's heel strike is the only hope of redeeming his people once and for all.

So he marches to the cross, bearing the shame and scorn of Jerusalem and the whole world, despised and rejected, a worm and not a man. The sun turns black, the earth shakes, and the Son of God, who holds the universe together, through whom everything was made, gives up his spirit. He dies. The King of Glory dies.

The Crazy Things We Do for Love

What a strange turn of events. God, in a whiff of thought and will, could have wiped the universe clean and started over again. But he didn't. Instead, he took our burden of shame and guilt upon his own shoulders, endured the scorn and humiliation of the cross, and died the death our sins deserve. What would motivate such radical, loving sacrifice?

The answer, in a word, is love. Love makes people do crazy things. The stories we tell in literature and film are full of examples of the crazy things people will do for love. Love empowers Odysseus through madness and suffering, driving him desperately and longingly back toward home. Love makes James Potter stand in front of Voldemort's killing curse to protect his wife and child, and gives his wife the courage to do the same. It sends Prince Phillip through a forest of thorns and into war with a dragon to rescue Sleeping Beauty. It's the motive behind a thousand songs and poems. It's woven into the fabric of our universe because it's reflective of the very heart of God.

Love is what sends Jesus into the humble estate of Mary's womb. It leads him through his quiet life, his rambunctious public ministry, and his agony at Golgotha.

Long before the birth of Jesus, God told Israel that they were his bride, and their failure and abandonment of him made them like a whoring wife. Through the prophets, we see the broken and grieving heart of God, saddened by the chaos and destruction of the wondrous world he created.

In Christ, that failed marriage became a success, because Jesus was willing to shed his own blood to preserve it. Paul tells us that somehow, in the mysterious foreknowledge of God, the very concept of marriage has *always* been a metaphor for the love of Christ for his church (Eph. 5:32). It was love for his promised bride that compelled him to the cross. "For God so *loved* the world . . ." (John 3:16).

The Song of Jesus

All of the sacrifices of the forefathers—the blood that flowed from their temple, that stained the doorways of Israel in Egypt, that poured out of the split carcasses before Abraham—all of it was a foreshadow and a preview of the shed blood of Jesus. Their songs of lament and longing were all sung in hazy anticipation of the song of Jesus, sung in the throes of death and under the weight of God's righteous and wrathful fury: "And about the ninth hour Jesus cried out with a loud voice, saying, 'Eli, Eli, lema sabachthani?' that is, 'My God, my God, why have you forsaken me?'" (Matt. 27:46).

Jesus was bearing both the physical agony of crucifixion and the spiritual agony of God's wrath. He'd been betrayed by his own follower, abandoned by his friends, and subjected to the worst kind of public humiliation. As his blood poured out and he drew nearer to death, he opened his mouth and cried out words he'd likely sung many times—the opening lines of Psalm 22.

It's a perfect song for the Savior to sing in that moment. For twenty verses of this messianic poem, the psalmist cries out in anguish as he's surrounded, tortured, and pierced through his hands and his feet. It's a chilling prophecy of the execution of Jesus. And then, in verse 21, the story changes. God intervenes and rescues the suffering one. "You have rescued me from the horns of the wild oxen!"

As soon as the psalmist acknowledges his rescue, he determines to call the nations to worship.

> I will tell of your name to my brothers;
> in the midst of the congregation I will praise you. (v. 22)

For the next ten verses, he sings a redemption song, inviting the whole world to join him and celebrate the God who saves. The suffering servant becomes a worship leader, inviting the world to come and worship the God who has rescued him.

The Torn Curtain

Moments after Jesus cries out those words and breathes his last, the temple curtain is torn in two (Matt. 27:51). That curtain wasn't mere furniture—it was a safety device, shielding the world from the consuming fire of God's presence. When it tears from top to bottom, it announces that God's presence is no longer confined to the temple. New access is provided for God's presence through the broken body of Jesus. The author of Hebrews quotes Jesus:

> Sacrifices and offerings you have not desired,
>   but a body have you prepared for me. (Heb. 10:5)

At the cross, Jesus offers himself as a substitute for us, taking upon himself the deadly wrath we deserve. In the aftermath, we're invited to draw near to God as never before.

> Therefore, brothers, since we have confidence to enter the holy places by the blood of Jesus, by the new and living way that he opened for us through the curtain, that is, through his flesh, and since we have a great priest over the house of God, let us draw near with a true heart in full assurance of faith, with our hearts sprinkled clean from an evil conscience and our bodies washed with pure water. (Heb. 10:19–22)

Jesus, the Temple

In a single event, Jesus revolutionizes worship. By offering his body as a sacrifice for us, he makes it possible for the unholy to enter the presence of the holy. The unimaginably wide gap between sinners and their Maker is bridged by the unimaginably worthy sacrifice of Christ on the cross. The temple—the intersection of heaven and earth—finds its new locus in the person of Jesus, the God-man. If you wanted to meet with God, you once traveled to a building. Now, you only have to look for Jesus. He once told a crowd, "Destroy this temple, and in three days I will raise it up" (John 2:19).

On the third day after breathing his last on the cross, he rises up from the grave, his resurrected frame a glorious new temple and a beacon to the whole world, inviting all who may come to worship the God who saves. Psalm 22, the song cried from the cross, concludes with this declaration:

All the ends of the earth shall remember
  and turn to the LORD,
and all the families of the nations
  shall worship before you.
For kingship belongs to the LORD,
  and he rules over the nations.

All the prosperous of the earth eat and worship;
  before him shall bow all who go down to the dust,
  even the one who could not keep himself alive.
Posterity shall serve him;
  it shall be told of the Lord to the coming generation;
they shall come and proclaim his righteousness to a people
    yet unborn,
  that he has done it. (Ps. 22:27–31)

"He has done it." God has kept his promises to Eve, Abraham, and all of Israel.

Jesus: Our Priest and Worship Leader

Not long after the resurrection, Jesus ascends to heaven, up through the clouds and into realms unknown to us. There he takes his place in the heavenly temple, at God's right hand.

If we're not careful, we might mistake the meaning of Jesus's ascension. It sounds kind of like a retirement send-off—like Jesus finishes his work and sits down to enjoy the fruits of his labor, but that isn't what happens at all. Jesus ascends to heaven to complete his work in transforming worship, standing in the presence of God as our perfect Priest.

The author of Hebrews tells us that the former generations of priests did their work imperfectly. They themselves were imperfect (Heb. 7:27), and they were destined to die, unable to escape the grip of the curse (Heb. 7:23). But Jesus is sinless and conquers death. "Consequently, he is able to save to the uttermost those who draw near to God through him, since he always lives to make intercession for them" (Heb. 7:25).

Other priests did their work with limited success, but Jesus is "able to save to the uttermost." He can finish what he starts in rescuing us.

Don't miss the significance of that last phrase: "he always lives to make intercession." Our Priest—Jesus, who is God himself—intercedes for us. He prays for you, and he does so with a perfect and compassionate understanding of our frailty and weakness.[2]

> Since then we have a great high priest who has passed through the heavens, Jesus, the Son of God, let us hold fast our confession. For we do not have a high priest who is unable to sympathize with our weaknesses, but one who in every respect has been tempted as we are, yet without sin. Let us then with confidence draw near to the throne of grace, that we may receive mercy and find grace to help in time of need. (Heb. 4:14–16)

In Christ, we are never alone, never misunderstood, never without an ally and a friend. The omniscient One who made the universe looks upon you with empathy and love and prays to the Father on your behalf. He prays for you and with you, and he invites you to join him as he worships the Father: "Now the point in what we are saying is this: we have such a high priest, one who is seated at the right hand of the throne of the Majesty in heaven, a minister in the holy places, in the true tent that the Lord set up, not man" (Heb. 8:1–2).

There at God's right hand, Jesus is serving as a "minister in the holy places." The language used here indicates that Jesus is leading a cosmic worship service, into which all who follow him are invited to participate.[3] This means that for every Christian, at all times and in all places, there has only ever been one Worship Leader, one who is worthy to enter that sacred space and able to endure the wrath of God in our places, making us able to "boldly enter in" with and through him. The songs we sing, the prayers we pray, the faith we confess—all of it is an echo and an amen to the perfect worship offered to God by his Son.

[2] Torrance, *Worship, Community and the Triune God of Grace*, 55–57.
[3] Kidd, "Jesus Christ, Our Worship Leader" (blog post).

One can imagine the strangeness of the moments after the ascension. Jesus's disciples are looking at the empty sky and pondering the whirlwind of the previous several days: Christ has died. Christ has risen. Christ will come again.

They journey back to Jerusalem and begin to pray, and the whirlwind kicks up again.

Pentecost: The Temple of God and the People of God

Jesus promised them a helper—the Holy Spirit—who would baptize them after he left. As they meet in the upper room and pray, the Holy Spirit is poured out, filling the disciples with power, wisdom, and authority. They become, as they are filled with the Spirit, the body of Christ on earth, a Spirit-filled temple of God. If "God dwells in Israel" was the declaration of Israel, then "God dwells in the church" is the declaration of Pentecost.[4]

Ever since Genesis 3, God has been at work restoring what sin had broken. The harmony of creation, the participation of God's creatures in the Trinity's glory-sharing life, is made anew because of Jesus. The Holy Spirit indwells the hearts of believers, who are led in worship by their High Priest and Mediator, Jesus, who reveals the Father to the church and represents the church to the Father. We worship the Father, through the Son, by the power of the Spirit. Worship is always and only participation in the life and work of our Trinitarian God.

The Spirit's indwelling presence makes the final transformation of worship complete. Now, once again, God's children can journey out to the corners of the world knowing that God is with them. "Or do you not know that your body is a temple of the Holy Spirit within you?" (1 Cor. 6:19). The relocation of the temple to Jesus expands, by the outpouring of the Spirit, to include the hearts of men and women. By the power of the Spirit, we're "in Christ" (Rom. 8:1; 1 Cor. 1:30), Christ is "in us" (Rom. 8:10; Gal.

---

[4]Simon Chan's discussion of the importance of Pentecost to understanding the role of the Spirit in worship is very helpful. See *Liturgical Theology*, 33–34.

4:19), and our life is "hidden with Christ in God" (Col. 3:3). Our life is a dwelling place for God.

The prophet Joel had a vision of this when he wrote,

> And it shall come to pass afterward,
>   that I will pour out my Spirit on all flesh;
> your sons and your daughters shall prophesy,
>   your old men shall dream dreams,
>   and your young men shall see visions. (Joel 2:28)

From Time and Place to Spirit and Truth

This, too, was foreshadowed by Jesus himself. In John 4, Jesus meets a Samaritan woman near a well.

> The woman said to him, "Our fathers worshiped on this mountain, but you say that in Jerusalem is the place where people ought to worship." Jesus said to her, "Woman, believe me, the hour is coming when neither on this mountain nor in Jerusalem will you worship the Father. You worship what you do not know; we worship what we know, for salvation is from the Jews. But the hour is coming, and is now here, when the true worshipers will worship the Father in spirit and truth, for the Father is seeking such people to worship him. God is spirit, and those who worship him must worship in spirit and truth." (John 4:20–24)

Her question has its roots in Israel's worship; the Samaritans and the Jews carried on a heated dispute over where God was properly to be worshiped. Jesus's response is to blow away her categories. Instead of worship being about time and place— the mountain or Jerusalem—it's about spirit and truth. For the apostle John, the word "truth" almost always is a reference to Jesus, who is "the way, and the truth, and the life" (John 14:6). His answer points to the radical transformation of worship that will occur in the aftermath of the cross and resurrection. The Father will be worshiped through the Son (the truth) by the power of the outpoured Holy Spirit.

Worship as Participation in the Life of the Trinity

For the church, then, worship is participation in Jesus's own worship of the Father by the power of the Spirit. It's initiated by the Spirit's prompting, made possible by the Son's work, and all about the Trinity's glory. We're invited in as participants and witnesses to that glory, and it's a glory that transforms us. "And we all, with unveiled face, beholding the glory of the Lord, are being transformed into the same image from one degree of glory to another. For this comes from the Lord who is the Spirit" (2 Cor. 3:18).

We're made more glorious as we participate in the glory-sharing life of God. There's nothing in the equation for which we can take credit—God initiates it through his Spirit, makes it possible through the Son, and glorifies himself in the process.

It's just like creation, wherein God made all things and they glorify him by the nature of their existence and participation in his work. Once again, the redeemed are *by their very nature* glorifying and worshiping God. This is why Paul calls us "living sacrifices" (Rom. 12:1) and God's *poiēma*, a word translated "workmanship" and related to our word *poem*. It indicates that in Christ, God has made us beautiful once again; our entire lives are an acceptable offering of worship, continually transforming, growing in our glorious reflection of his own nature.

At the center of this new world of worship is Jesus himself, who has made it possible and whom the Father glorifies as a result. Philippians 2:1–11 tells of Jesus, enthroned in glory, making himself a servant, accomplishing God's redemptive purposes on the cross, and being exalted above everything in heaven and on earth. His life of unbroken and perfect worship is the means by which we all can join the song, and because the Father has given him the "name that is above every name" (v. 9), the song we sing glorifies him.

In Christ, the song of the patriarchs and of Israel comes to a triumphal completion. Like the beautiful movement of Psalm 22, the longing of the patriarchs, the weary blues of the wilderness, and the tear-filled lament of the exiles find themselves resolving into a glorious celebration hymn in the life, work, and song of Jesus. That's the story of worship: God creates, sin corrupts, but Christ redeems. And all of us get to sing along.

Chapter 5

WORSHIP ONE, TWO, THREE

The story of the gospel is all about worship. God has done radical and surprising things in order once again to provide a way for his children to live in community with him. The harmony of creation is restored through the church, in whom God's Spirit dwells. By that Spirit's power and through the way made by Jesus, we enter the presence of the Father.

So how does this relate to what we call worship in the local church? How are we to think about gathering with the people of God today, and what are we to make of the promises that are yet held forth—best of all, that one day Christ will return?

Singing in Exile

Theologians have long talked about how life in the church is a life of "already and not-yet" realities. We are already saved from the guilt, shame, and wrath deserved by our sins, but not yet free from their snare upon our lives (Romans 7). The world is being made new by the work of the gospel (Rev. 21:5), but that work is yet incomplete (Rom. 8:22). The church is victorious (Rom. 8:37), yet it suffers persecution, illness, and death (Rom. 8:36).

One way to think about this already and not-yet worship life of the church is through the metaphor of exile. In 2 Kings 24, the Babylonians attack Israel, seizing its leaders and dragging them off to another land. There, God's people are surrounded by a hostile Babylonian culture, a pluralistic society that frowns on their religion and wants to pressure them to assimilate. But Israel was a people formed with a promise. Even in exile, the promise is held forth that God will rescue them, and that in the meantime he means for them to worship him, hold on to the promise, and receive blessing from him (Jeremiah 29).

The church, similarly, is a community in exile. We're challenged to be in this world but not of it. We're called to thrive where we are and hope for our future. Our song is sung in the tension of life between this world and the one to come, where all things are restored and sin is abolished once and for all.

Confusion Abounds

Even so, when we talk about worship today, confusion abounds. One person uses the word to describe a particular style of music. Another uses it to describe a formalized liturgy, vestments, candles, and incense. Still another talks of worship as a way of life. And in between these varied definitions, debates rage.

Many of us grew up in churches that went through years' worth of worship wars, where the piano-and-organ crowd battled for control of the church platform with the guitars-and-drums crowd. Conversations about worship get loaded with emotion and weighed down by preferences. One crowd laments the lack of depth in the lyrical content of our songs, while another laments the lack of contextualization and stylistic flavor.

Whole movements emerge arguing that worship should be shaped by the evangelistic mission of the church, and thus our services need be "attractional" and friendly. Others swing the pendulum the other way, arguing that worship is only about the church gathering and worshiping their God, and that outsiders shouldn't even factor into our planning for the gathering.

So who's right? Who has the weight of the Bible on their side? What should worship look like among the exiles who enjoy God's grace here and now, yet suffer with sin and its destructive consequences, all while eagerly anticipating Christ's return?

Here's an attempt to answer that question.

Worship One, Two, Three

Like any challenging topic for the life of the church, much centers on our definitions. So far we have described worship as ascribing worth to God by participating in his own glory-sharing life. That took a particular shape in Eden, another shape in Israel, and yet an altogether new shape in the life of the church. To describe that worship life in the church, I want to suggest a framework I call Worship One, Two, Three. By unpacking this, I think we'll have some helpful guardrails for understanding worship and church life.

Simply put, Worship One, Two, Three is this: worship has

- one object and author,
- two contexts,
- three audiences.

Once defined, this framework can answer a lot of the questions, confusion, and challenges that come up when we talk about worship in the church.

One Object and Author

The object is the easiest and most obvious place to start. The story of worship makes it clear: God is at the center of all of our worship. He is the single most glorious thing in the whole universe, the One to whom we ascribe the greatest and highest worth. By this, of course, I mean God the Trinity—the Father, Son, and Holy Spirit, who are three but one, sharing and exchanging glory in a dance beyond our imagination.

Out of that loving community, God created the world—authoring all of creation's responsive declarations of his glory. When sin corrupted that world, he promised to come and redeem it. God declared his own centrality to worship in the Ten Commandments (Ex. 20:1–5) and again and again made clear that he would not share his glory with another (see, for example, Isa. 42:8; 48:11). As redemption history unfolded, he lifted up the Son as the central figure of worship and glory in all of creation (Phil. 2:1–11; Col. 1:5–20), who in turn, proclaimed the glories of the Father (John 14:13).

God created worship, and created it anew in Christ. So not only is he the supreme object of all of our worship and praise; he's also its author, giving us life and breath, vision and redemption, eyes to see, ears to hear, and mouths to declare his goodness and glory. Worship is about God, from beginning to end.

Two Contexts

Participating in God's glory-sharing life, then, happens in two contexts: scattered and gathered. Worship scattered is the Spirit-filled life of the Christian in the world, and worship gathered is the meeting of God's people to remember, encourage, and bless one another.

Worship Scattered

First, worship scattered. This broad, life-filling reality is the way things were meant to be when the world was made, a way of intimacy and community that was restored by Jesus, who tells us to boldly enter God's presence (Heb. 4:16) and cry out to him with the intimacy of his child (Rom. 8:15). Because we are united with God in Christ, our whole lives are now caught up in Jesus's cosmic worship of the Father, and we once again participate in the glory-sharing life of God. As Harold Best describes it:

> Nonetheless, this singular fact, full to the bursting, remains. It is a fact grounded in infinite outpouring: Christ is in me; I am in Christ. . . . Christ in me is not some narrow, introspective, disembodied, private, even embarrassing fact, specially savored by a narrow sect within the larger Christian community. It is an all-encompassing, all-empowering fact from which no quarter of my worship can be excused.[1]

This means that, for the Christian, whatever you are doing—whether serving the poor in Guatemala, serving Communion in a

---

[1] Best, *Unceasing Worship*, 57.

local church, flipping hamburgers in a diner, or flipping channels on TV—it all happens in union with Jesus, before the eyes and presence of a loving God, who by a miracle of boundless grace receives each and every act, though offered with mixed motives or frailty of heart, as a pleasant and acceptable offering.

Scattered worship reveals the scandal of God's grace. The whole mess of our lives is transformed in Christ, from corrupted to glorious, from ashes to beauty. The addict who can only cry out in miserable faith, "Lord Jesus, have mercy on me, a sinner," is just as accepted by the Father as a faithful missionary or a clean-cut-Christian celebrity pastor. There are no mountains to climb to seek God's presence, no gates to unlock, no feats to accomplish. There is only Jesus, who throws wide heaven's gates and cries, "All who are thirsty, come and drink" (see John 7:37).

He extends that invitation to you and me. Draw near. Walk behind the curtain. Behold God's glory as you live out your days. Unrestricted access is yours in Jesus. Worship, as Jesus told the Samaritan woman, no longer has an address. It's about a man named Jesus, who has given us more than we dared dream.

Worship Gathered

This invitation will sometimes tempt us to wonder why the church still has worship services. If worship is spirit and truth, not time and place, and is fully accomplished by Jesus, then why does the church still gather?

The author of Hebrews offers an explanation. After describing the priesthood of Jesus in the heavenly realms (Hebrews 8) and his once-for-all sacrifice (Heb. 9–10:18), the author then invites us to draw near to God through Jesus (Heb. 10:19–22) and to continue to gather.

> Let us hold fast the confession of our hope without wavering, for he who promised is faithful. And let us consider how to stir one another to love and good works, not neglecting to meet together, as is the habit of some, but encouraging one another, and all the more as you see the Day drawing near. (Heb. 10:23–25)

Through the book of Hebrews, we're shown how Jesus replaces the central focus of Israel's gathering—the temple, the priest, the sacrifice—and yet the author goes on to tell his readers to continue to gather. The gathering's purpose shifts from the work of the priests—the efforts to cleanse Israel's sins—to the work of the church—encouraging one another, and all the more as "the Day" approaches.

The "Day" here is the day of judgment. The passage goes on to warn of the dangers of falling away, and the author points to the gathering of the church as one key for holding fast under the pressures of a broken world and the temptations to sin.

This is familiar territory when it comes to the story of worship. We're profoundly forgetful creatures, and the consequences of forgetting our God are frightening. Adam and Eve forgot God's word in the garden, and the Devil, the world's first heretic, twisted their judgment and led them down a path toward death. Ever since, the authors of the Scriptures have been crying out warnings for us to remember, to guard our hearts and protect ourselves from forgetting:

- "Take care, lest you forget the covenant of the LORD your God, which he made with you, and make a carved image, the form of anything that the LORD your God has forbidden you" (Deut. 4:23).
- "Take care lest you forget the LORD, who brought you out of the land of Egypt, out of the house of slavery" (Deut. 6:12).
- "You shall not forget the covenant that I have made with you" (2 Kings 17:38).
- "The wicked return to Sheol, / all the nations that forget God" (Ps. 9:17).

We continue to gather in the light of this profound weakness. Like the children of Neverland, we're forgetful, or "prone to wander," as the old hymn says. Worship scattered happens in the midst of a not yet restored world, where those around us have long forgotten their Maker. Their idolatry—their love of money, fame, and glamour—is like the pagan Asheroth totems that dotted the land-scape around Israel. We, like them, are quick to forget our God and quick to install the totem in our living rooms, revolving our lives around it. Our only hope is to remember the gospel—remembering who we are and whose we are as we rehearse the story of redemption that calls us out of the wilderness and back to the garden.

Who Came to Church?

It's no small thing to realize that when a Christian shows up, God shows up. "Do you not know that you are God's temple and that God's Spirit dwells in you?" (1 Cor. 3:16).

So when the church gathers, it gathers as a collection of people in whom God dwells. God inhabits the gathered church because these scattered worshipers are all temples, who together make a greater temple.

> So then you are no longer strangers and aliens, but you are fellow citizens with the saints and members of the household of God, built on the foundation of the apostles and prophets, with Christ Jesus himself being the chief cornerstone, in whom the whole structure, being joined together, grows into a holy temple in the Lord. In him you also are being built together into a dwelling place for God by the Spirit. (Eph. 2:19–22)

When this temple gathers, something otherworldly takes place. It's an outpost of hope in a dying world, a fellowship of resurrected sinners, whose presence in the world is a foretaste of a greater transformation to come.

> And he gave the apostles, the prophets, the evangelists, the shepherds and teachers, to equip the saints for the work of ministry, for building up the body of Christ, until we all attain to the unity of the faith and of the knowledge of the Son of God, to mature manhood, to the measure of the stature of the fullness of Christ. (Eph. 4:11–13)

Theologian David Peterson points out the communal nature

of the text[2]—Paul is talking about the formation of an entire church, not just individuals. It's not merely that *I* should be built up, but that *we* should be built in unity. This happens as those given to lead the church exercise their gifts, teaching and preaching from God's Word.

> . . . that we may no longer be children, tossed to and fro by the waves and carried about by every wind of doctrine, by human cunning, by craftiness in deceitful schemes. Rather, speaking the truth in love, we are to grow up in every way into him who is the head, into Christ, from whom the whole body, joined and held together by every joint with which it is equipped, when each part is working properly, makes the body grow so that it builds itself up in love. (Eph. 4:14–16)

"Speaking the truth in love" is often understood as saying hard things or dealing with conflict: we "speak the truth in love" when we confront sin or say unpopular things lovingly. According to Peterson, though, "speaking the truth in love" is not so much about interpersonal boldness as it is about a community that shares a confession, a unified expression of faith in the God who saved them.[3] The gathered body teaches the Word and proclaims it together; we speak the truth in love as we sing, read the Scriptures, and remember the gospel together.

The Goal of the Gathering

These passages, taken together, show us a church that gathers in the midst of the world's pressures, under the hopeful warning of Christ's return, encouraging one another and building each other up through the presence of God's Spirit by immersing itself in God's Word, singing and proclaiming the gospel. The fruit of the gathering is not just a strong individual, but a strong church, united in faith.

In this sense, the gathering is unique not as an encounter

---

[2] Peterson, *Engaging with God*, 209–10.
[3] Ibid., 209.

with God (it is that, though God's presence is a constantly available comfort and help to the Christian); rather it's unique because it is an encounter with the people of God, filled with the Spirit of God, spurring one another along in the mission of God. Christ in me meets Christ in you.

It's not just a family reunion, either. We gather because we have work to do—to remember the gospel and hold fast to our confession. The Greek word for the gathered church offers some insight into how the apostles saw their gatherings. Though the language offered a variety of options for words to describe the gathering church, the authors of the New Testament chose *ekklēsia*. According to scholar Larry Hurtado, it was an odd choice: "In its historic Greek usage, *ekklesia* designated the gathering of citizens of a city to *conduct civic business*. Such events always had a religious character and would be commenced with offerings to the gods, but the *ekklesia* was not precisely a gathering to conduct worship."[4]

We gather because we have work to do. *Ekklēsia* emphasizes *the work of the people*. We gather to do our work, which is to say, we gather to remember, to encourage, and to spur one another on.

Scattered and Gathered . . . Together

Gathered worship then feeds scattered worship, building up and equipping worshipers to live in the power and wonder of the gospel, able to persevere amid the trials that surround them. Likewise, scattered worship feeds gathered, as each worshiper brings his or her growth, suffering, and maturing faith to the gathering. Harold Best beautifully shows the connection between the two contexts of worship:

> We must conclude that the Christian needs to hear but one call to worship and offer only one response. These come exactly coincident with new birth and, despite our wanderings and returns to the contrary, they suffice for all our living, dying, and

---

[4] Hurtado, *At the Origins of Christian Worship*, 54–55, my emphasis.

eternal outpouring. We do not go to church to worship. But as continuing worshipers, we gather ourselves together to continue our worship, but now in the company of brothers and sisters.[5]

Colossians 3:16–17 has this same paradigm:

> Let the message of Christ dwell among you richly as you teach and admonish one another with all wisdom through psalms, hymns, and songs from the Spirit, singing to God with gratitude in your hearts. And whatever you do, whether in word or deed, do it all in the name of the Lord Jesus, giving thanks to God the Father through him. (NIV)

Verse 16 describes the heart of the gathering—singing, sharing, and encouraging one another that the word of Christ might dwell richly among us. Verse 17 then opens the doors to the wider world, inviting us to step out with thankful hearts, doing everything in the name of Jesus. Worship scattered and worship gathered go hand in hand, shaping and informing one another in the life of the worshiper. One without the other will inevitably be weakened.

It's a gospel rhythm—sent and gathered, always worshiping and regularly worshiping together, with the story of the gospel throbbing in regular rhythms at the heart of the church: this is who you are, this is your God, this is your story. It's a life-giving and community-building pulse, and when the gospel is at the center—remembered, declared in unity, and displayed in the church's worship—it's a rhythm of grace.

Three Audiences

None of this happens in a vacuum. These rhythms of scattering and gathering happen before many watching eyes—the audiences of worship. In the era of the rock-star worship leader, the word *audience* might come across as part of the problem. Worship should be for God's sake, right? It isn't about the crowd we draw, is it?

---

[5] Best, *Unceasing Worship*, 47.

The Scriptures make it very clear that there are many eyes on the people of God, both as they gather to worship him and as they live their lives in scattered worship. In this sense, we can talk about worship having an audience—the eyes that witness the worshiping church.

In fact, there are three distinct audiences that the church needs to be aware of, both gathered and scattered. There is God, who is both the object of our praise and a witness to us as we praise him; there is the church, which both participates in and witnesses the lives and gatherings of the people; and there is the world, watching from the darkness.

God as Our Audience

God's presence as an audience reminds us that our worship isn't called out from another room. It's not a Skype call. We don't have to shout for him to hear us, and we don't have to get the "recipe" right for him to pay attention. God is here, now, wherever a believer calls on his name. Not only that, he calls and accepts us just as we are because he meets us through Jesus, whose work makes us presentable. The Maker of heaven and earth is *always pleased with us because of Jesus.*

This isn't to say that all of our methods are stamped "approved," or that what we're doing when we gather is always wise. Rather, it's simply to state that worship done humbly in Jesus's name is received with joy by the Father. We needn't fear our acceptability or lack thereof. We need only trust in Jesus as we gather and scatter.

It's sometimes overwhelming to think about preaching, or leading worship, or even showing up at church. We imagine this gathered body to be a special, holier-than-I bunch. We fear that the moment we enter the room, someone will discover that we're faking it, we're impostors, and we'll be kicked to the curb. The gospel tells us just the opposite. It reminds us that this gathering is always made up of sinners saved by grace—nothing more and nothing less. It reminds us as well that the hard work is already done. The sins we abhor have been fully paid for by Jesus. And finally, it tells us that the most important audience member is completely pleased with us in Jesus.

All this is to say that having God in our audience means there is One who accepts us just as we are and deems our imperfect worship as made perfect in Jesus. When you worship, seek him out, and let his assured presence, peace, and comfort be foremost in your mind. These things in combination with his power and majesty bring comfort without complacency, the thrill of God's presence rather than terror. "Let us offer to God acceptable worship, with reverence and awe, for our God is a consuming fire" (Heb. 12:28–29).

> In the fear of the LORD one has strong confidence,
> and his children will have a refuge. (Prov. 14:26)

The Church as Our Audience

Which brings us to the next audience member: the church.

Many a young worship leader (or worship enthusiast) has commented, "We shouldn't sing songs *about* God; we should only sing songs *to* God." Similarly, some may say, "All these songs that talk about us—they're man-centered, and worship should be God-centered. Let's not sing about us. Let's only sing to God."

This sounds pious and high-minded until you realize how many of the psalms are singing about and to Israel. Several New Testament passages thought to be early hymns of the church are the same way; they're declarative and confessional, rather than directly addressing God. This becomes even clearer when you read passages like Colossians 3:16 and Ephesians 5:19, and you realize that Paul's command is to sing to *one another.*

The Bible makes it very clear that the church is an audience of worship and that the purpose of the gathering, in many ways, speaks to this audience. As I said earlier: the gathering is unique not as an encounter with God (since God's presence is a constant comfort and help to the Christian); it's unique as an encounter with God intensified among the people of God, filled with the Spirit of God, spurring one another along in the mission of God. It's communal, not individualistic. Christ in me meets Christ in you. The gathering should be a place where believers are built up and encouraged in the midst of the various trials and circumstances of their lives.

So when we gather, we sing to each other. We declare the truths of the gospel to one another. Our presence and our participation is not merely for the sake of our individual relationship with God, demonstrating our confidence and hope, but it's also for our brothers' and sisters' sake. Our participation in the gathering is testimony and encouragement to them. When you sing, you are "speaking the truth in love" to your church around you, and your bold confession of faith may be exactly what someone nearby needs to hear in the midst of his or her dark hours. Likewise, you may be the one who needs to receive the comfort that comes from the praises of God's people.

The Watching World as Our Audience

These bold declarations have yet another audience: the watching world. As the church gathers, it proclaims to the surrounding world that Jesus is King, that he alone saves, and that he is their only hope. Just as the Psalms declare the wonders of God to all of Israel, they declare them to the nations (Ps. 96:3). In the New Testament, we see the gathered church as an island of exiles whose worship causes outsiders to see Christ's glory and be drawn in. Paul, in 1 Corinthians 14, admonishes the church to seek to prophecy more than they seek the gift of tongues. He describes an outsider at a gathering: "The secrets of his heart are disclosed, and so, falling on his face, he will worship God and declare that God is really among you" (1 Cor. 14:25).

It's the clarity of prophecy—heart-cutting words in an intelligible tongue—that makes the moment transformative for the unbeliever. Tim Keller says:

It cannot be missed that Paul directly tells a local congregation to adapt its worship because of the presence of unbelievers. It is a false dichotomy to insist that if we are seeking to please God we must not ask what the unchurched feel or think about our worship. . . . God wants the world to overhear us worshipping him. God directs his people not to simply worship, but to sing his praises "before the nations." We are not to simply communicate the gospel to them, but celebrate the gospel before them.[6]

This reminds us of the centrality of the gospel to the gathered church. As Keller says, the world needs to clearly and coherently see the gospel celebrated. Even though three audiences witness our worship, the message doesn't have to be tailored separately; all of them need to see and hear the gospel displayed and celebrated.

Confusing the Categories

Taken together, Worship One, Two, Three is just shorthand for understanding where we are in the story. A day will come when those realities will change once again, but until then, we worship scattered and gathered, with the church, before the eyes of the watching world.

You'll find that many of the heated battles of the worship wars erupt when these categories get confused. For instance, the well-intentioned seeker-sensitive movement seems to have lost sight of the church as an audience in worship (and a crucial one). Those who would rather lie in bed and watch The Masters on Sunday have lost sight of the call to gather with God's church. Those who compartmentalize their "church" life from their hellish "secular" life forget that they are living sacrifices, and all of life is an act of worship.

Most errors in the church come not from outright lies, but from subtle distortions. Often, they come when a good thing is exaggerated and made into everything. Worship has been a con-

---

[6] Keller, "Evangelistic Worship." The same can be said of scattered worship—the world witnesses how we live out and celebrate the gospel. Our authenticity, our love for one another, our glory-transformed lives of worship are evidence of its power and truthfulness (John 13:35).

tentious issue for as long as the church has been gathering, and most of us have witnessed battles in our churches. While some of these conflicts are silly, such as fighting over the color of drapes or the length of the Communion hymn, many are far more serious.

Confusing the Object and Audience

One of the greatest areas of confusion is the distinction between the audiences and object of worship. As already mentioned, there's an occasional tendency to think that gathered worship is only "for the audience of one," only about "me and Jesus." At one level, this results in some silly decisions—singing only *to* God, or making worship a purely vertical encounter. But the natural progression of such a thought can lead into much more dangerous territory.

For instance, worship that's intended for God's attention alone doesn't need to be comprehensible to anyone but an all-knowing God. Language can become dense and archaic in the name of honoring God's holiness and transcendence. The actions of worship leaders and pastors in a gathering can become utterly indiscernible, the gathered church can become spectators, and the watching world is alienated.

In one stream of church history, this can help explain worshiping in a dead language like Latin—holy language that honors God but leaves the church bewildered. It's believed that the incantation "hocus pocus," spoken to convey magical transformational powers, is derived from "Hoc est enim corpus meum," the Latin phrase meaning "This is my body," uttered by Roman Catholic priests during the Eucharist (the Lord's Supper) in the Mass. The confused congregation heard these "magical" words and believed that they transformed the bread and wine into Jesus's body and blood.[7]

In another stream of history, a confusion of audiences may explain the wild and disorderly charismatic experiences of the church at Corinth (see 1 Corinthians 14 again) and the absurdities

---

[7] Tillotson, *The Works of Dr. John Tillotson*, 443. I first heard of this from Kevin Twit.

witnessed during the Toronto Revival in the 1990s—people bark-
ing like dogs, people stuck to the floor in "Holy Spirit glue," and
"holy laughter." This madhouse cacophony is more easily justified if worship is all "between me and Jesus," but the gathering
is meant to be orderly, clear, and comprehensible by insiders and
outsiders. God, after all, is a God of order and peace (1 Cor. 14:33),
and his desire for our gatherings is that they would build up and
encourage his church, not bewilder us.

Overemphasizing Contexts

Similarly, the way we understand the contexts of worship can
cause deep confusion. I've already mentioned the idea of scattered
worship as an excuse for sleeping in on Sundays. Just as dangerous
is the notion that the gathering is the only place where worship
really happens.

Such an attitude loads up the worship service with burdens it
simply can't carry. When a one-hour worship service is our *only*
encounter with God's presence, we will intuitively become much
more demanding of that gathering—and divisive. Song selection,
for instance, is a much more loaded concept if Sunday morning is
my sole sacred hour with God. I'll be much more picky because
a decision I disagree with or don't particularly love robs me of
intimacy with God. A brokenhearted friend who asked me for
prayer would be guilty of pulling me away from the Holy of Holies. Everything about the service becomes sacred, and if it's done
poorly (or not to my taste), it's not just a matter of preference or
opinion—it feels more like heresy.

By contrast, if the gathering is about building up and encouraging the church, then a song I don't like presents an opportunity
to love and encourage others whose tastes differ from mine. A
needy friend is an opportunity for me to participate in the work
of the church (the *ekklēsia*), listening, praying, and building him
or her up. Distractions, errors, and cringe-inducing moments in
the service aren't disasters on a cosmic scale because worship con-

tinues throughout my week; Jesus continues before God's throne, and I can join him anytime.

Overemphasizing Audiences

Audiences, too, can lead to overemphasis. The seeker movement sought to reshape worship gatherings toward unbelievers in a way that removed any and all roadblocks. Critics of the movement accused its leaders of removing the offense of the gospel, attempting to make Christianity "cool" or more easily palatable by watering down truth.

While any generalization is, by its nature, going to be too broad (surely some compromised and some didn't), it's clear that the seeker movement overemphasized outsiders at the expense of insiders. Gatherings became spectator events with flashy music and theatrical performances, an hour and a half of entertainment for the sake of winning people to the faith. This isn't to say that the gospel wasn't presented or proclaimed—surely it was—but the gathering wasn't aiming to build up and strengthen the church as it lived out the gospel in the midst of evil days.[8]

Other churches so emphasize the building up of the church that they become downright hostile to outsiders. Lengthy and incomprehensible sermons and songs, unexplained practices like giving and Communion, holy-huddle cliquishness, and deep immersion in the Christian cultural ghetto combine to make outsiders feel like uninvited guests at a family reunion.

If we're honest about our churches, we'll find that the need for coherence isn't only for outsiders. Our churches are full of people who have been well versed in church vocabulary and long disconnected from its real meaning and impact on their lives. The presence of unbelievers reminds us that we need fresh, conversational, and comprehensible language to explain why we're gathering and what we're celebrating, and that emphasis can help

---

[8] Some, recognizing this weakness, launched weeknight services that aimed at building up the church, and that's certainly an admirable approach, though in the light of the biblical picture of the gathering and the history of the church, it feels a bit backwards.

ignite renewal among believers who've grown cold to church-speak and Christianese.

The Message for All Audiences

The encouraging thing, in the light of these tendencies toward exaggeration and overemphasis, is that the cure is the same: the gospel. The gospel is all about once-broken worship being restored by Jesus. We worship the Father with and through the Son by the power of his Spirit. The gospel transforms all of life into sacred space because Christ dwells in us and we dwell in him, and this frees us from expecting too much from the gathering and yet compels us to gather and encourage one another.

Worship that celebrates the gospel brings all three audiences together: the God who saves by the gospel, the church formed by the gospel, and the world in need of the gospel. We're often tempted to move on to other messages, to move past the gospel into more "mature" topics of the faith, but we never get "past" the gospel because we never get past the need for Jesus to mediate between God's holiness and our sin.

In fact, ever since Genesis 3, worship has always been about the gospel. In Israel, it was foreshadowed by priests and sacrifices. In the church, we have the joy and privilege of seeing it fulfilled in Jesus, and at the end of time, the heavenly city gathers around a throne room, worshiping the Lamb who was slain. Throughout history, worship has been a wonder-filled response to the God who made a way to rescue us.

Chapter 6

WORSHIP AS SPIRITUAL FORMATION

In most conversations about worship, an obstacle stands in the way: you. Whether you know it or not, intend it or not, you carry a deep well of ideas about what worship is, what it looks, sounds, and feels like. You've built this knowledge over the years and decades of your life, adding to it each time you've gathered with the church. One might say, "I don't really have a theology of worship," but in fact everyone does. That's because we are habit-formed people.

Shaped by Habits

Notice I say "habit-formed" and not "habit-forming." We are formed by the habits in which we live.

Imagine that you'd never heard of softball. One day, someone at work invites you to go play the game with a group she gathers with weekly. You accept the invitation and go, excited to learn about this strange, unknown game.

You're taught the rules, and after a few Saturdays, you begin to actively participate and contribute to the game. Months go by, and one day someone new comes to the game. At first, he's excited to be playing. "I played softball for years back in Michigan," he says, but he's quickly troubled. On your team, the bases are run clockwise. You pitch the ball to yourself. And every home run is met with a rousing chorus of "God Save the Queen."

Things gets really difficult when your friend attempts to help you reform the game by the actual rules, and not the Marx Brothers–inspired farce in which you currently participate. Running counterclockwise is dizzying, and everyone finds himself swinging wildly at slow-pitched balls. The song is still sung on occasion, but its meaning is long gone.

The habits of your corrupted version of softball shaped the way you understood and participated in the game. Anything different was difficult to comprehend, and only after immersion in new habits over a long period of time would you begin to appreciate them.

It works the same with worship. Our worshiping habits have shaped our understanding and our expectations. Most of us have positive emotions attached to the way we regularly gather with our churches, and shifting those ideas (and eventually, shifting those habits) comes painfully. This is why the "worship wars" of a few years ago were so intense. The habits of traditionalism were ingrained, connecting with powerful emotions of joy and meaningfulness. Singing contemporary praise choruses instead of hymns and listening to preachers in polo shirts instead of suits felt a lot like running around the bases backwards.

I say all this because I want to make some specific arguments about what the church should do when we gather in the light of the gospel. I will inevitably offend some of you, and for that I am sorry. But I'm also certain that it's worth reconsidering many of the ways we think about gathering with the church.

To be clear, though, I am not saying that everyone else's worship is a Marx Brothers–inspired farce. Far from it! What I am saying is that our ways of gathering are deeply ingrained habits, and their habitual nature makes it difficult to see alternatives as viable. So I challenge you to suspend your suspicions and follow me down this path for the next few chapters while exploring what, for many of you, may be a different world.

Forming Habits That Form Us

So I want to begin by talking about our habit-formed lives. Nearly everything we do that's important to us is learned through practice. No one sits down with a cello and immediately plays Bach's Suite No. 1 for Cello. It takes years of practice to cultivate the sense of intonation and timing, the hand strength and touch sensitivity, not to mention the basic rudiments of reading and studying music. This need for time and practice is true of anything—public speaking, athletics, and creativity of all kinds. To learn any of these skills, one must develop habits and routines that make for progress. We are literally training our bodies to cooperate with us as we seek to live them out, which is why athletes and musicians talk about "muscle memory."

We do this because we believe the reward of our efforts is great enough to justify the required sacrifice of time and effort. Some skills, like playing golf or painting with oils, take little time to learn the basics and thousands of hours to master—if mastery is even achievable. We form habits, like practicing for an hour a day or visiting a driving range once a week, and our habits form us, ingraining the correct angle of a swing or the shape of our hands over the keys of a piano.

Worship as a "Thick" Habit

Philosopher James K. A. Smith, in his fascinating and helpful book *Desiring the Kingdom: Worship, Worldview, and Cultural Formation*, distinguishes between practices that are thin (and less meaningful, like brushing our teeth) and thick (more meaningful, teaching us to love and desire deeply, and shaping identity). In the thick category, Smith locates our specific religious habits, like worship and daily devotions, as well as more incipient habits, like extended TV viewing or listening to inflammatory talk radio for three hours a day.[1]

It's in this framework that we need to think about corporate worship. Gathering with the church is a habit we form, and it's a "thick" habit, one that profoundly forms us. As I said earlier, a wellspring of experience from years of worshiping together has formed all kinds of ideas about what worship is, who God is, and

---

[1] Smith, *Desiring the Kingdom*, 82–83. Smith's work has been a huge influence on my own thinking about worship, and much of it bleeds through this chapter and the following.

what it means to be the church. For good or bad, our worship practices are forming us and our communities, giving shape to what we believe.

A church that gathers each week with cold seriousness, lofty architecture, dense language, and grumpy upper-middle-class white people is making a statement about the kingdom. Those who congregate there weekly are being formed into a kind of community. Likewise, a church with smoke, lights, rock-star worship leaders, and celebrity pastors is forming a particular kind of community. How we gather shapes who we are and what we believe, both explicitly (through the actual content of songs, prayers, and sermons) and implicitly (through the cultural ethos and personas).

The ancient church summed this up in the Latin phrase *lex orandi, lex credendi*, which essentially means "so we pray, so we believe." The phrase acknowledges this habit-formed reality. The identity of the church is formed and transformed as it gathers around the Word and responds in the songs, prayers, and fellowship of the saints.

So let's all acknowledge this fact: for better or worse, our worship, regardless of our tradition or musical style or culture, is shaping the hearts and minds of our congregations. We are always teaching, shaping, and painting a picture of what the Christian life looks like. It's in this light that we should evaluate our gatherings. What are we saying about "normal" Christianity? How do our services reflect the way the gospel changes our perspective on the world? What are we saying to those who suffer? To the poor? The rich? Those who are like us? Those who are unlike us? How are we connecting to past, present, and future?

Different Visions for the Gathering

In any given community with multiple churches, you will find varying answers to those questions. In one, the church gathers with a weightiness and austerity, reading Scripture, singing hymns, and listening as the organ echoes off the rafters. In another, things are much more casual, the music rambunctious, with the whole service seeming more vaguely "inspired by" the Scriptures than grounded in them.

These differences don't exist without conflict. During much of my childhood and teenage years, I watched a church transition from piano-and-organ gatherings to full-band, nearly charismatic gatherings. The conflicts were tense and bitter, and many church members were wounded in the process. I remember three rows of older members standing up, fingers in their ears, and walking out during a rousing special music performance of Stephen Curtis Chapman's "The Great Adventure."

I'm a guitar player, and I lead a ministry that does edgy, contemporary music. So I don't want to give the impression that I'm a grumpy traditionalist. Nonetheless, one has to ask, how did we get here? How did we get to a place where "worship" is so dramatically varied? In the midst of all the conflicts about style, culture, and content, who has it right? We know that worship is both scattered and gathered, but what exactly is the goal of that gathering? And what are we actually accomplishing with the practices in place, given that we are inevitably shaping hearts and minds as we gather, and what are we *meant* to accomplish?

What makes answering this question difficult is how vague the New Testament is when it talks about the gathered church. The cosmic scale of New Testament worship is crystal clear; our songs (and our very lives) are caught up in the worship service Jesus is leading in the true tabernacle. We see the mechanics of that worship service in technicolor—the blood of Jesus making a way for us to enter in; the Son of God leading us in a procession from captivity to new homes in the kingdom; the tribes, tongues, and nations gathered before the throne of God. But Sunday morning gets much less vivid illustration. In stark contrast to the particularity of Old Testament temple worship, New Testament gatherings seem open-ended. We're invited to participate in a variety of ways, but with far less austerity.

It's clear that worship begins and ends with the gospel. It's the gospel of God's generous grace that makes boldly entering into God's presence possible, and when we gather, we celebrate that gospel, encouraging one another and preparing one another to be sent back out into the world on a gospel-fueled mission. Our story as God's people is now intimately tied to the gospel story.

Worship, Story, and Covenant Renewal

Our gatherings are meant to connect us to one another and to the story God is telling in history, and to spur us on toward our hope-filled future. While the particulars of worship in the New Testament are radically different from the patterns of the old, the centrality of God's redemption story is a point of wonderful continuity. Israel was a story-formed community, and their gatherings were punctuated by remembering God's story and their place within it. Where the church's worship is centered on the cross and resurrection, Israel's story centered on their own rescue: the exodus. Throughout the Old Testament, when you see the people of God gathering, you see them remembering their story. When God introduces himself in conversation, he says, "I am the LORD your God, who brought you out of the land of Egypt." The identity of Israel and the terms of their relationship with God are firmly and thoroughly rooted in their history. So every time they get together, they recount their story and their place within it, rehearsing and reaffirming their identity.

In Joshua 24, Israel's prophet-leader gathers the people to call them back to the God who saved them. He begins by retelling their story (vv. 1–13) and then says, "Choose this day whom you will serve" (v. 15). Joshua presents worship as a choice between the God of Israel and the idols of the world around them. Their task is not only to worship the Lord; it's also to reject their idols. The people respond, and Joshua presses in, warning them that worship calls for the wholesale rejection of their lesser gods (vv. 19–23). The gathering climaxes as the decrees and laws are reaffirmed (v. 25) and the covenant is renewed.

Theologian John Witvliet, commenting on this passage, says:

> This particular narrative emphasizes several aspects of Israel's covenant liturgy that stand in continuity with Christian practice: The assembly gathers self-consciously *coram Deo*, before the face of God, for a corporate action, with no mention of those who dissented or did not feel like making the vow (v. 1). The current covenantal vows are set in the context of the narrative of God's saving activity (vv. 2–13). Human speech is received by the gathered community as divine discourse (note the attribution of divine discourse in vv. 2–13). A vow of fidelity to God is a resounding no against all false gods (vv. 14–15). The assembly is gathered not for the purpose of learning or even prayer but for making a vow to serve God (vv. 16–24).[2]

Throughout the Old Testament, a similar pattern of covenant renewal is repeated. The Word is presented, reminding people of their God and their story, the people repent, and the covenant is reinvigorated with fresh commitment on behalf of the people of God (see also 2 Kings 23; Nehemiah 8–10; Deuteronomy 31). Witvliet continues:

> The covenant language does not end with the advent of the New Testament age. Rather, Scripture challenges us to see that in Christ, God has extended a new covenant promise to the church (Jer. 31:31–34; 2 Cor. 3:6; Hebrews 8–9). Recall all the places in which marriage is a metaphor or image to describe the church's relationship with God (Isa. 62:5; Jer. 2:2; Hosea 3:1; Rev. 19:7; 21:2, 9).[3]

Our commitment to the gospel is reaffirmed as we gather with the church and remember God's promises to us.

> Just as the people of Israel gathered together to renew their covenant with God (i.e., Josh. 24:1–27), so we Christians gather to renew the new covenant God has made with us in Christ. Christian worship is like a covenant-renewal service in which the

---

[2] Witvliet, *Worship Seeking Understanding*, 30.
[3] Ibid.

gathered reaffirm the vows made with God in Christ. . . . In a worship service, we renew the promises we made (and often failed to keep) to God, and we hear again the promises God has made (and kept!) in Christ.[4]

A gathering with this purpose—remembering and renewing our commitment to God in the light of the gospel—is driven by a profound sense of purpose. Remember that the New Testament word used to describe the gathered church (*ekklēsia*) indicates a gathering with purpose. We come with work to do: remembering and renewing our covenant. This stands in contrast to the way many of us view the gathering. Witvliet comments:

> The pastoral question we face is whether most people experience worship this way or whether, in contrast, they really experience it as a meeting of a religious social club, or an educational forum, or a form of entertainment. Because these other kinds of events are common in our culture, we are bound to take our expectations for them with us into worship. In contrast, worshipers need to be challenged to see the worship event as a deeply participational, relational event in which we are active listeners, speakers, promise receivers, and promise givers.[5]

It's similar to when a married couple renews their vows. They aren't inaugurating something new when they look into one another's eyes and reaffirm their love for each other. Instead, they're saying, in the light of all that's happened in their years of marriage, that they remain committed to one another. In a worship gathering, when the church comes together to hear the gospel afresh and respond in faith, it's a similar reaffirmation. God's promises still stand, and we remain his people by faith.

Concert Hall versus Banquet Hall

My friend Isaac Wardell, a pastor of worship and founder of Bifrost Arts, asks whether we think of gathered worship as being more

---

[4] Ibid.
[5] Ibid.

like a concert hall or a banquet hall.[6] If it's a concert hall, we show up as passive observers and critics, eager to have the itches of our preferences and felt needs scratched. A banquet hall, by contrast, is a communal gathering. We come hungry and in community, ready to participate and share the experience with one another.

In the New Testament, the glimpses we're given of the gathered church are very much like the banquet hall, or perhaps even the potluck. The church comes together with the expectation of participating by giving and receiving. There's an expectation that members gather with work to do. From a wide-angle lens, we see them meeting to remember the gospel and spur one another along. Zooming in more closely, we see a variety of ways that purpose is carried out:

- prayer with and for the community (Acts 2:42; 1 Cor. 14:16; 1 Tim. 2:1)
- reading the Scriptures (Col. 4:15; 1 Thess. 5:27; 2 Thess. 3:14; 1 Tim. 4:13; 2 Pet. 3:15–16)
- preaching from the Scriptures (Luke 4:20; 1 Tim. 4:13; 2 Tim. 3:15–17; 4:2)
- serving the Communion meal (Acts 2:42; 20:7)
- singing psalms, hymns, and spiritual songs (1 Cor. 14:15; Eph. 5:19; Col. 3:15–16; Rev. 5:9–13)
- giving offerings for the poor and the mission of the church (2 Cor. 9:11–15; Phil. 4:18; Heb. 13:16)
- confessing their faith (1 Tim. 6:12; 1 Pet. 3:21; Heb. 3:15)
- giving and receiving God's blessing (Luke 24:50; 2 Cor. 13:14)
- greeting one another (Rom. 16:16; 1 Cor. 16:20; 2 Cor. 13:12; 1 Thess. 5:26; 1 Pet. 5:14)
- responding to praise and prayer with the saying of "Amen" (Rom. 1:25; 1 Cor. 14:16; Eph. 3:21)[7]

Theologian D. A. Carson points out that these purposes are what make the worship gathering of the church unique. While there's no doubt that all of life is caught up in Jesus's work and

---

[6] Lucke and Wardell, "Is a Worship Service More Like a Concert Hall or a Banquet Hall?" (blog post).
[7] Adapted from a list compiled by Edmund Clowney, as cited by Carson, *Worship by the Book*, 48.

worship, there's something uniquely edifying about the church when it gathers for Scripture, song, and the Communion meal— something different from what happens when people (for example) take a sewing class together.[8] The express purpose of such a gathering, the unique centrality of the gospel to what is said and done, sets it apart from ordinary life. God's indwelling Spirit is at work as we sing, preach, and pray his Word, and it's transformative of the congregation.

Theologian Jeremy Begbie calls the gathering an "echo from the future,"[9] a foretaste of something we'll see come to fruition when Christ returns and all things are made new, a not-yet life that we taste in part already. Today, we gather in exile, in the world but not of it, but one day the exile will end. God will rebuild creation, and not one corner of it will be stained by sin and rebellion. Until then, we have these momentary and imperfect glimpses and foretastes as we gather, hear the Word, and respond together. As flawed and imperfect as these gatherings are, they're the most truthful moment of our week, an outpost of the kingdom of God and a foretaste of eternity.

The Gathered Church and Spiritual Formation

Carson notes how many of the activities are connected in one way or another to the Word, either directly (reading, preaching, praying, and singing) or indirectly, as responses to the Word (confessing faith, saying the "Amen").[10] Larry Hurtado, in his excellent short book *At the Origins of Christian Worship*, points out how this Word-centeredness was a stark contrast to the religions of the world around the early church. The pagan religions of Rome were sensual, with ceremonies, orgies, statuary, and a vibrant visual culture.[11] Yet the church gathered simply, centering their collective life on the Word of God and the community's participation. Their goal was to

---

[8] Carson, *Worship by the Book*, 48.
[9] This quote is from Begbie's plenary lecture, "Re-Timed by God: The Rhythms of Worship," at the Calvin Symposium on Worship, January 2010.
[10] Carson, *Worship by the Book*, 48.
[11] Hurtado, *At the Origins of Christian Worship*, Kindle edition, location 127.

shape the hearts and minds of Christians, following on the heels of
Deuteronomy 6:7, saturating the life of the believer with the Word
of God as it was read, preached, prayed, and sung. It was profoundly
countercultural in Rome to gather so simply and starkly.

The earliest church gatherings were still in the temple and
synagogues, and the synagogue in the first century was itself a
Word-centered, soul-forming place. Robert Webber describes worship in the synagogue as being a Word-centered event in which
the counterculture of Israel was taught and reaffirmed through
affirmation of faith, prayer, and the reading of Scripture.[12] They
gathered to remember the covenant, pray together, and hear the
Word read and taught.

It was in this environment of Word-centered community that
the early church sprung its roots. Jesus grew up in the synagogues,
and much of his teaching ministry occurred in synagogues outside
of Jerusalem. To grow up there was to have your worldview and
life shaped by disciplined immersion in God's Word. In this world,
the gathering wasn't an event designed to wow or impress. You
didn't attend as a spectator. It was a place you entered to have your
identity formed and refined as part of God's community, living
under the testimony and authority of God's Word. Gathering with
God's people was part of an identity-shaping rhythm of life.

This rhythm remained in the aftermath of the resurrection
(Acts 2:46; 3:1; 5:42). Believers continued to meet regularly in the
temple and in public. Where the center point of God's saving work
had been the exodus, in the light of the empty tomb it became the
work of Jesus. The gathered church meets with the same agenda:
remember and celebrate how God rescued us, pray and sing in
community, hear and respond to the Word.

Worship as Protest

The broader context of the worshiping church provides the best
lens for understanding the purpose and goal of the gathering. Just

---

[12] Webber, *Worship Old and New*, Kindle edition, location 555.

as Israel met in the temple and synagogue, testifying to the world that there was only one God, resisting the pressure to conform to the pluralism and decadence of Babylon, Syria, and Rome, we worship the Savior while surrounded by a fallen world and myriad fallen voices. They call to us, luring us with the false promises of other gods and saviors: money, sex, power, success, relationships, and fame; and in their very midst, we remember Jesus, the firstborn of the new creation, and declare that we live for another King and another kingdom.

Psalm 121 is a psalm of ascents—a prayer sung by pilgrims on their way to the temple in Jerusalem. The psalmist sings,

> I lift my eyes up to the hills.
> From where does my help come? (v. 1)

The mountains on the road to Jerusalem were littered with temples and idols, little gods who offer protection from bandits and thieves on the journey.[13] The threat of attack would tempt weary travelers to go to the mountains, worship one of these lesser gods, and trust in it to save, but the psalmist refuses.

> My help comes from the Lord,
> who made heaven and earth. (v. 2)

This is what we do every time we gather with the church. We not only affirm that our hope is in him; we deny any hope in the gods of the world around us. As Jean-Jacques von Allmen says:

> Every time the Church assembles to celebrate the cult, to "proclaim the death of Christ" (1 Cor 11:26), it proclaims also the end of the world and the failure of the world. It contradicts the world's claim to provide men with a valid justification for their existence, it renounces the world: it affirms, since it is made up of the baptized, that it is only on the other side of death to this world that life can assume its meaning. . . . Christian worship is the strongest denial that can be hurled in face of the world's

---

[13] Peterson, *A Long Obedience*, 40–41.

claim to provide men with an effective and sufficient justifica-
tion for their life. There is no more emphatic protest against
the pride and the despair of the world than that implied in
Church worship.[14]

The Real Worship Wars

Whoever dubbed the debate over musical style a "worship war"
failed to realize that worship is always a war. The declaration that
there is one God, that his name is Jesus, and that he has died,
has risen, and will come again is an all-out assault on the saviors
extended at every level of culture around us. We're taught to find
a sense of hope in a political party, trusting in our duly elected
saviors to make the world right once and for all. We're taught to
find our identity in our friend counts on Twitter or Facebook.
We're taught that a victory at work or good news from a doctor or
a bathroom scale will satisfy us. We look longingly into the eyes
of other human beings and believe that they can affirm us enough
and love us well enough to end our sense of loneliness.

We believe these things because we've been taught them again
and again. Like the ascending pilgrims of Psalm 121, we're surrounding by clamorous mountains advertising happiness, sex,
and power, all available for consumption. Our entertainment in
television, film, and literature paints the good life this way, and
it grips our heartstrings, calling us away to worship at the feet of
these idols.

James K. A. Smith identifies this phenomenon when he says:

> It is not primarily our minds that are captivated but rather our
> imaginations that are captured, and when our imagination is
> hooked, we're hooked. . . .
>
> This is just to say that to be human is to desire "the king-
> dom," *some* version of the kingdom, which is the aim of our
> quest. Every one of us is on a kind of Arthurian quest for "the
> Holy Grail," that hoped-for, longed-for, dreamed-of picture of
> the good life—the realm of human flourishing—that we pursue

---

[14] Quoted in Chan, *Liturgical Theology*, 42.

without ceasing. Implicitly and tacitly, it is such visions of the kingdom that pull us to get up in the morning and suit up for the quest.[15]

Worship isn't merely a yes to the God who saves, but also a resounding and furious *no* to the lies that echo in the mountains around us. The church gathers like exiles and pilgrims, collected out of a world that isn't our home, and looks hopefully toward a future. Our songs and prayers are a foretaste of that future, and even as we practice them, they shape us for our future home.

---

[15]Smith, *Desiring the Kingdom*, 54.

Chapter 7

WORSHIP AND THE STORY OF THE CHURCH

Two thousand years is a long time. Jerusalem is a long way from North America. Somehow, in that span of years and distance, the church's gatherings have adapted from meetings in synagogues to austere and elaborate liturgical services in iconic cathedrals and the high-dollar productions of North American megachurches.

Some of these changes are merely cultural, like the style of music and the manner of gathering, but some are philosophical and theological. Not all churches meet for the same reasons and expectations. It's helpful to know a little bit of history in order to understand how we got here. Such an effort, in the space we have here, is going to be limited—but my goal is to hit a few highlights (and perhaps to encourage you to read more on the topic). With a clear picture of where we've been and how we've arrived here, I think we can better answer the questions above.

The Shifting Life of the Church

For the early church, its exclusive hope in Jesus became a catalyst for persecution, and Christians were forced to scatter. Their gatherings became more secretive in their hopes of staying alive. They had to leave the temple and synagogues, and eventually they had to go underground altogether. Brave souls were marched to the edge of town and stoned. Some were taken to the coliseum, where they where fodder for maddened crowds who watched them torn to pieces by animals, crucified, and otherwise tortured and dismembered for the entertainment of the mob. Their public witness was shaped by the hope of the martyrs, who trusted in Christ as death bore down upon them through man and beast. Despite the best efforts of Roman emperors like Nero, Trajan, and Marcus Aurelius, the church survived. It eventually even prevailed.

In 313, the emperor Constantine issued the Edict of Milan, ending persecution against Christians and legalizing the practice of all religions throughout the empire. During his reign, Christianity spread like wildfire throughout Rome, and Christianity quickly grew to be the most powerful and influential religion in the empire. Christians went from gasping for air under the fire of persecution to having the official religion. The church spread far and wide. Authority in the church centralized in Rome under the leadership of Gregory the Great, and thus the papacy was born, and the church became an institution in an entirely new way.

Over the generations that followed, the church became a hierarchical political power. The gospel became clouded and buried behind a church bureaucracy, a dead language, and a new priesthood. The unfettered access given to the church by Jesus was distorted, and mysticism and religiosity characterized the church for hundreds of years.

This happens over and over in church history. There's gravitation away from the gospel, a tendency to couch it in man-made structures and hierarchies, to hide it behind cultural hedges, or to trade in the grace of Jesus for a less scandalous system of religion. It happened as early as the age of the New Testament writers, when the Judaizers infected the Galatian church. It happens now too.

It's tempting to skip straight to the Reformation, to the efforts of men who brought the gospel and worship back to ordinary people. But first, I want to mention a couple of things about the legacy of the darker years in between. It's easy to look at this history purely through our own post-Reformation eyes. We see power consolidation under the pope as an unfortunate affair, but in its day, it preserved the church against the momentum of Gnostic and docetic heretics, who undermined the doctrine of the Trinity.

To many Protestants, the church calendar may seem like an arbitrary regulation, a testimony to authority and micromanagement
from Rome, but for its authors, it was designed pastorally. The
church calendar was designed to walk believers through the story
of the gospel every year, from the incarnation to the ascension. If
we allow historic prejudice to color our perspective too heavily,
we lose sight of the brilliant, pastoral creativity that shaped some
of the church's inventions.

Worship Confused

The error, of course, was to elevate ecclesiastical authority to
equal footing with Scripture. The church calendar, as a pastoral
and contextual concept for teaching people to live in the gospel
story, is a great idea. As a binding regulation ordered with abso-
lute authority, it distorts the purity of worship given to us by Jesus
and the authors of the New Testament. Likewise, creeds, confes-
sions, and orders of worship, when seen through the lenses of
gospel-given freedom, represent an opportunity to connect with
the past and acknowledge, as we gather with God's people, that
we're not the first ones to discover and love the gospel. When
they are mandated steps for finding acceptance by God, we end up
confusing the gospel and worship. Worship is an opportunity af-
forded through the mercy of Jesus, who met all the requirements
of the law and leaves us liberated from the burden of getting it
right in order to stand in the presence of God. In the light of that
fact, we need to be wary of anyone who offers us three easy (or
ten complicated) steps to God's favor and fellowship.

In those dark years, the gospel became veiled behind the trap-
pings of religiosity and a profound distinction between clergy and
laity. Worship was hierarchically controlled by religious officials,
and the actions of the gathered church became more divided between the clergy and laity. More of the work was done by the
priesthood, and the church itself became passive observers. Services weren't for the sake of mutual encouragement and blessing.

They were the means of salvation in and of themselves. One had to attend the service and participate in the Mass—the Catholic name for the worship gathering—to have any assurance of God's mercy. The priest, in serving and praying over the Communion meal, or Eucharist, was facilitating "transubstantiation"—the transformation of bread and wine into the actual body and blood of Jesus.

In the eyes of the church, the meal was itself a sacrifice, made by the priest on behalf of the people for the sake of satisfying the wrath of God. As one might imagine, church rulers became very powerful during this era. The clergy literally held salvation in their hands, and submission to the priest was an essential part of religious obedience; he took over mediating between God and men.

Imagine being a Christian in the year 1400. Worship services were in a language you didn't speak, and your vague comprehension of the gospel would be based upon the little understanding passed on to you by others or discerned from the Mass you attended. You would passively observe the clergy as they sang (you weren't allowed to sing), and you would listen as they read Scripture and carried out various rituals on an altar at the far end of a cathedral. At some point, they would serve the Eucharist through a mysterious set of actions that led to your only real participation in the service—taking a bite of bread and a sip of wine from the hands of a priest.

Throughout this era, voices of protest emerged. Movements sparked up seeking to bring renewal or to point to another way, but for nearly a thousand years these movements failed, ending with men and women being martyred for the sake of the gospel. Power remained consolidated and the gospel remained hidden.

The Reformation

In 1517, Martin Luther nailed his Ninety-Five Theses to the door of a church in Wittenberg, and a fire was lit that would transform churches the world over. The Protestant Reformation brought Scripture back to the people of God and with it restored a biblical vision of worship. As Luther once said regarding worship, "We can spare everything except the Word. We profit by nothing so much as by the Word."[1] The Bible was translated into the native languages of the people, and worship gatherings in new, Protestant churches were full of prayers, songs, and sermons in the vernacular. The Word was made central to the life and worship of the church, and everything else that was done in the gathering was reformed and reinterpreted in the light of God's Word—including the Communion meal.

The gospel began to spread and revival broke out in Europe. It was a return to the life-shaping rhythms of grace that punctuated the early church's (and Israel's) gatherings. Instead of a mysterious fog of religion, the clarity of the gospel was stressed again as God's people imbibed in his life-giving and soul-shaping Word.

The Free Church

In England, the Reformation had its own flavor. King Henry VIII had led the charge to separate English churches from Rome. After he was denied a divorce, Anglicanism was born in 1534.

Like the Roman Church, the Anglican Church had a strict hierarchy attached to the king, and it regulated the worship of local congregations with the Book of Common Prayer.[2] Behind this was an understanding that the church was under the authority of the crown—an idea that many Christians resisted in the wake of the Reformation around the globe. The "nonconformists" fought the hierarchy and (at various times) suffered greatly for it. For them, authority was ultimately in the Bible. It was an offense to have the state (or the bishop) tell them what Scriptures to read and preach and how worship was meant to be carried out each week. Their resistance gave rise to the Free Church (free from the regulations of the crown), the Puritans (a purified church), and

---

[1] Thompson, *Liturgies of the Western Church*, 98.
[2] While the demand that the Prayer Book be used universally is regrettable (to say the least), it is worth mentioning that the book itself is a great work of the Reformation, making worship comprehensible and providing a framework for shaping the Christian life with a breadth of Scripture, history, and prayer.

the Congregationalists (a church ruled locally, autonomously, by the congregation). These movements eventually gave rise to the Presbyterians, Baptists, and many of the streams of contemporary evangelicalism.

When we look at most of the modern trends in worship (especially in North America)—from the gospel music of the Gaithers to the Passion Tours—we find their roots here, in the Free Church tradition. Pastor and theologian Kent Hughes identifies the distinctives of the Free Church as follows:

- preaching—weighty expositional preaching (as opposed to short homilies)
- Scripture—reading long passages of Scripture (as opposed to piecemeal reading from the Prayer Book)
- prayers—lengthy, pastoral, extemporaneous prayers (as opposed to short collects and litanies)
- singing—congregational singing of hymns (as opposed to professional choirs)
- sacraments—a weightier treatment of Communion and less ritualistic ceremony for baptism
- simplicity—less ornate architecture and less ceremonial services
- rejection of vestments—robes and priestly garb viewed as counterintuitive to the new covenant[3]

A Scripture-alone approach went a long way to strip the gathered church of ceremony and tradition, allowing the glorious centrality of Jesus to shine. John Owen, one of the titans of this Reformation movement, said of Jesus in worship, "He freed them, by his teaching, from the bondage of Pharisaical, arbitrary impositions, delivering their consciences from subjection to any thing in the worship of God but his own immediate authority."[4]

The nonconformists believed that leading gathered worship was a pastoral task. In the Anglican Church, the entire worship gathering was dictated by the Book of Common Prayer—the se-

---

[3] Adapted from R. Kent Hughes, "Free Church Worship: The Challenge of Freedom," in Carson, *Worship by the Book*, 145–46.
[4] Owen, "A Discourse Concerning Liturgies and their Imposition," in *The Works of John Owen*, 15:4.

lected Scripture readings, the prayers, and the sermon (which was just a small homily, read from the book).[5] The nonconformist movement spawned countless seminaries and academic institutions because they believed that the pastor should be well equipped to preach the Word of God and shepherd his people. It gave birth to the hymns of Isaac Watts, John Newton, William Cowper, and all of the great English hymn writers. These men (and women like Anne Steele) wrote with a heart for shepherding and catechizing—training people in doctrine and a biblical worldview—through the songs they sang. Their legacy continues to be heard in the music of churches all over the world hundreds of years later.

Revivalism

Freedom from the hierarchy was liberating, but not without consequences. Over time, as Hughes points out, "Free Church biblicism deteriorated into Free Church pragmatism."[6] Revivalism, led by nineteenth-century preacher Charles Finney, transformed worship from the banquet hall to the concert hall. Rather than worship being a formational process in the lives and hearts of believers over years of gathering and learning, it became an ecstatic experience driven by emotive preaching and decorated with music. The goal was a catalytic, life-changing moment. According to Hughes:

> The structure of corporate worship became: (1) the preliminaries, (2) the sermon, and (3) the invitation. . . . Singing and musical selections were made in regard to their effect rather than their content. Gospel songs (celebrating experience) often supplanted hymns to God. Scripture reading was reduced so as not to prolong the "preliminaries." Prayers were shortened or even deleted for the same reason. As to the sermon, the careful interaction with the biblical text so treasured by the Puritans was in many instances replaced with a freewheeling extemporaneous discourse.[7]

---

[5] It's interesting to me to think about the Prayer Book in the light of the current debate around video venues. The logic connecting the two is similar: use technology (printing in the sixteenth and seventeenth centuries, video now) to spread the Word.
[6] Hughes, "Free Church Worship," in Carson, *Worship by the Book*, 147.
[7] Ibid.

For many Christians in the years since, this has been the norm. Worshiping with the gathered church is about music and preaching, with preaching taking a central (and often primary) place, while music serves as an emotional warm-up. Preaching itself has devolved from the careful exegesis of the Reformers to vaguely Christian platitudes and techniques for self-help. Elements like prayer, Scripture readings, and greeting one another are seen as peripheral, decorative, and secondary to the real purpose of the gathering. In this economy, worship is defined as music, and its value is measured in its emotional impact more than its truth content.[8]

Historically, this idea is a big disconnect. The synagogue was a place where the people of God gathered to immerse themselves in the Word and be shaped by it. From that life-changing culture, the church emerged. Believers gathered to continually remember the gospel, to be nourished by God's Word, and to encourage one another. During the Reformation, that vision was restored, making Scripture comprehensible and enabling the congregation to participate actively in the gathering. But revivalism rewrote the script again. Worship became a momentary experience, as music and preaching led the congregation through a journey to conversion or repentance.

Worship after Revivalism

From there, a variety of streams and traditions developed. Driven by an emphasis on experience, whole traditions emerged from the preferences of particular congregations. Worship wars were often style wars, pitting generations against one another not because of philosophy or theology, but because of culture. Musical styles changed and evolved because experientially they worked better.

Some, recognizing a lack of clarity about the purpose of the gathering, have sought to understand the emotion-driven movement of post-revival worship in a theological framework. Many

---

[8] Rienstra and Rienstra, *Worship Words*, 235–36.

have embraced what's sometimes called the Temple Model (or the Wimber model, given its usual attribution to John Wimber, founder of the Vineyard movement of churches). This model likens the journey of worship to a pilgrim's journey to the temple in Jerusalem. As one worship leader describes it, "We see the 'Temple journey' of worship from every day life, walking towards Jerusalem, into the Temple courts and finally into the deepest place of God's presence."[9]

The journey begins in the "outer gates," where the crowd assembles rambunctiously, with celebrative and energetic music. As worship continues into the inner gates and into the temple, music becomes more intimate and the presence of God becomes more immanent. The goal of worship is to enter the Holy of Holies, where God's presence is most profoundly known and experienced. Once there, we sing only ballads and hymns, with tears streaming down our collective face.

Directly and indirectly, much of the church has embraced this model. It's been advocated by worship leaders like Judson Cornwall[10] and Andy Park.[11] It's also present in the way we talk about worship experiences, saying of worship leaders and teams, "They really led us to the throne room," or, "They ushered into God's presence."

The problem with this model is twofold. First, it's developed backwards. The theology of the Temple Model is a theological interpretation of an experience, and it is divorced from any kind of historical perspective on the gathered church. Second, it ignores most of what the New Testament teaches us about worship, the presence of God, and the temple. Instead of being led by Jesus through the inner curtain, we're led there by a worship leader or a pastor—a pseudo-priest. God's presence is measured in emotional impact, and it's mediated through music and preaching, displacing Jesus from his role as our sole Mediator and worship leader.

---

[9] Beeching, "My Top Tips on Creating a Set List for Worship" (blog post). Vicky Beeching is a CCM (contemporary Christian music) artist who primarily records worship music.
[10] Webber, *Worship Old and New*, Kindle edition, location 2341.
[11] Park, *To Know You More*, 68–69.

Common Ground: Revivalism and Roman Catholicism

Frankly, this isn't far removed from the errors of Roman Catholic worship. Both revivalism and Catholicism measure the presence of God through the work of the church—the Communion service in one, music in the other. Both install a new priesthood responsible for leading the people to God and speaking for God to the people. In Catholicism, he wears vestments and doles out God's presence in bread and wine, and in contemporary worship, using the Temple Model, he wears a fauxhawk hairstyle and an acoustic guitar.

It's interesting, too, to see that Roman Catholic worship, by making the cathedral a place where priests serve and heaven comes to earth, is itself modeled after the temple. Somehow, both in historic Catholic worship (and, for that matter, it's theological cousins in Anglo-Catholic and Orthodox churches) and in contemporary, experience- and emotion-driven worship, we are seeking to recreate a temple experience, mediated by human beings who lead us to an experience of heaven on earth that the New Testament tells us is profoundly inferior to worshiping the Father through the Son by the power of the Spirit. It's not unlike in the book of 1 Kings, where the people of Israel have God as their King in an arrangement that makes them unique among the nations. Even so, they aren't content and they demand a human king. God gives them Saul, David, and Solomon, who despite their better achievements, are profoundly flawed. So it is with any human priest or mediator: we reject Jesus, our worship leader, and settle for Saul.

None of this is to say that worship isn't meant to be experienced emotionally, or that the quality of experience and production in our gatherings is unimportant. Far from it. But what drives us? What do we consider the most important? What do we consider success? Do we think about our gatherings as catalytic, or cumulative? Are we looking for explosive, instantaneous impact or gradual, steady life change? Is it a concert hall or a banquet?

We come to our churches eager to hear deep truth and connect spiritually with our communities and with God. For many in North America, that quest ends at a gathering led by celebrated pseudo-priests who guide us through a fine-tuned emotional roller coaster. They lead us to "the throne room" and back, and invite us to come back next week for more of the same. Such a gathering paints a distorted picture of the kingdom of God, shaping hearts and forming identity via a heavy (if not exclusive) reliance on emotion, technology, and celebrity to do so.[12]

But it's not the way to gather. And that's not to say that technology, culture, and emotions are evil. In fact, a faithful presentation of the gospel and the God of the Scriptures should result in an emotionally charged response. The Spirit of God has a tendency to do powerful things when Jesus is on display and when God's people gather. That's a powerful recipe for life-changing worship: gather the people of God, display the glories of Jesus, and invite the church to respond.

We have to see that there's a difference between a service that's compelled by a hunger to display the gospel and a service that's compelled by a desire to stir emotions through other means. We also have to see that the church needs to be equipped for more than emotional catharsis. In the chapter that follows, we'll explore some of the other habits that the church has cultivated historically and how they influence us for everyday life.

For now, it's important to remember the gospel even as we reflect on the efforts of worship leaders. As Harold Best says, "we offer, Christ perfects." Our best efforts to worship in spirit and truth, feeble or confused as we may be, ascend to the heavens through faith in Jesus. They're cleansed by his blood, and they arrive at God's throne a perfect, pure, and fragrant offering.

I thank God that's true for me.

---

[12] In the ongoing discussion about celebrity pastors and celebrity worship leaders, we should consider the formative power of our worship services. Perhaps people idealize pastors because they've been formed to do so, week in and week out, for decades.

Chapter 8

LITURGY AND THE
RHYTHMS OF GRACE

In the last few years, there's been some buzz about liturgy.[1] Ministry buzz, of course, is nothing new, and the conversations I've been a part of regarding liturgy aren't unlike conversations about fad words like *missional* or *emergent* from a few years ago. There's nothing new under the sun. The word *liturgy* can be confusing, often conjuring up images of "smells and bells," vestment-wearing pastors and priests, burning incense, and ancient chants.

The word itself comes from two Greek words meaning "public work," or (as it's often described) "the work of the people." To talk about liturgy in its most basic sense is to talk about what the congregation is gathering to do. In this sense, every church has a liturgy; we all gather with work to do. At one end of the spectrum, that liturgy might be extremely loose—a general mood set through songs and pastoral leadership; the "work" to be done is a powerful emotional experience. At the other end of the spectrum, the liturgy might be detailed in a word-for-word script that walks the congregation through a collection of prayers, songs, and Scripture readings.

It's through our liturgies that the rubber of *lex orandi, lex cre-*

---

[1]See, for instance, Mark Galli, *Beyond Smells and Bells*, which advocates the "wonder" and "power" of liturgy, and *The Accidental Anglican: The Surprising Appeal of the Liturgical Church*, by Todd Hunter, a former Calvary Chapel and Vineyard pastor. Mainstream megachurches like Savannah Christian Church have experimented with liturgical services, and churches like The Journey in St. Louis, Missouri, and my own church, Sojourn Community Church, in Louisville, Kentucky, have at various times had liturgical services. The most recent Sovereign Grace Worship Conference (Worship God 2011) was called "The Gathering" and was built around an exploration of the liturgy as described by Bryan Chapell, *Christ-Centered Worship*.

dendi (so we pray, so we believe) hits the road. As we plan and order our services, discerning the content to include, we shape the beliefs and devotional lives of our church members. It's a crazy pastoral opportunity, if you think about it. When else do you have the opportunity to put words in people's mouths? As Debra and Ron Rienstra point out their book, *Worship Words*:

> In a fundamental sense, worship language, like all of worship, is *formative.*
> The words we hear, sing, and speak in worship help form
>
> - our images of God;
> - our understanding of what the church is and does;
> - our understanding of human brokenness and healing;
> - our sense of purpose as individuals and as a church;
> - our religious affections: awe, humility, delight, contrition, hope;
> - our vision of wholeness for ourselves and all creation;
> - our practices of engaging with God, with each other, and with the world.[2]

As we're singing and praying, we're incorporating the truths of these songs and prayers in our hearts. Truth is simultaneously taught and put into action. John Witvliet describes it this way:

> Worship both presents concepts and "practices" concepts. For example, we hear repeated references—and perhaps an occasional explanation—of the Trinity, but we also experience prayers offered to the Father, through the Son, in the Spirit, prayers that invite us to imagine God as the One who is before us, alongside us, and within us.[3]

Taught and Caught

Beliefs are both taught explicitly (through sermons and teaching) and caught implicitly (as congregations participate in the prayers and songs of the church, which are themselves loaded with affir-

---

[2] Rienstra and Rienstra, *Worship Words*, 28.
[3] Abernethy, *Worship That Changes Lives*, 49.

mations and denials of beliefs). Consider the way children learn to talk. Notice how they imitate the sounds they hear. The same thing is true of us as we learn to pray. We begin with imitation, copying the phrases and ideas that we hear in the community around us. Soon, these become more and more personalized, until we have a freedom and dexterity in prayer to improvise, which feels wholly personal and unimitative. Listen carefully to the language in a Bible study or prayer group that has been together for a while, or listen as various pastors pray in your church. How do they ask God to heal someone? How do they confess their sins? How do they praise and worship God in prayer? How do they present needs and requests? You'll hear common phrases, common themes, even common rhythms and patterns of speech. What they share through a common language is far more significant than what separates them.

You'll notice it in yourself if you ever join a new church, or if your church brings in a new pastor or worship leader. The language of new leaders and pastors will inevitably, unintentionally transform the way you pray and think about God outside the gathering. It's an entirely unconscious process. No one is telling you or anyone else to imitate others, but the process of imitation, personalization, and improvisation holds true for anything in life. We pick up nuances from others and make them our own. Even efforts that begin as highly self-conscious and deliberate acts, like throwing a baseball or sketching, become, through regular practice, habits of mind and body in such a way that they are almost reflexive—instantaneous and natural.

Relationships depend on this kind of disciplined learning too. My marriage grows deeper and richer as I deliberately seek to learn how to love my wife well. This means practices like listening, repenting, speaking words of affection, and deliberately seeking to do acts of service for her. I don't merely need to speak, but I need to learn to speak *to her*. There is a difference between saying something and saying it in a way that your spouse hears, understands, and affirms. These practices in a marriage may at first seem challenging, and our flesh will want to resist them, but with regular practice, they become habits of mind and body—easier, more natural, and more joyful. Likewise, as I seek to know Jesus more intimately and more seriously, I must engage in practices that make hearing his voice and acknowledging his lordship and my weakness more deeply ingrained into the habits of my mind.

Pastoral Responsibility

For pastors and leaders, this reality should make us shudder; our decisions about the practices and rhythms in our church gatherings are forming the character, beliefs, and devotional life of those who attend. Eugene Peterson has said that the primary task of the pastor is to teach people to pray.[4] In a recent "Q Session" with Gabe Lyons, he described how church members would ask him to help them learn to pray, and he'd answer by describing a group that gathered weekly to do just that—and would they like to join? Inevitably they'd say yes, and Peterson would invite them to their regular Sunday morning worship service.

Our gathering, learning, and practicing happens in community. Gathered worship is where the unity of Ephesians 4 is most clearly expressed when, as one body, we affirm one Lord, one faith, one baptism, one God and Father of all (Eph. 4:5–6). It's also the most significant furnace of Ephesians 4:11–16, where those gifted to shepherd God's church are said to build up the body through the gifts he's given them as they build up the body in unity and faith, and we all "speak the truth in love," declaring and remembering the gospel in community, abounding in love for God and one another.

The inverse is true too. If we are feeding on a steady diet of spiritual junk food, moralistic triumphalism, and pop psychology, we're going to be malnourished. The contemporary praise movement has long been critiqued for its tendency toward happy-clappy victorious pop songs and its failure to speak to the darker

---

[4] Peterson, *Under the Unpredictable Plant*, 111.

side of Christian experience. Harold Best once commented that the contemporary praise movement had virtually nothing to say in the light of 9/11 and Katrina.[5] The large bulk of its songs have focused on the celebratory and the triumphant. When faced with terrible national and global tragedy, the community and the collected "canon" of songs didn't have the language to adequately respond. This is a bad place for the church to be. If our worship gatherings are formative of our beliefs and are teaching us to pray, then we need to embrace practices that prepare us to respond faithfully to life's storms.

This brings me back to liturgy. The goal of our gatherings should be to cultivate practices that form our church to live in the good news of the gospel. The primary concept we "present and practice" (to borrow Witvliet's language) should be the gospel. Nothing better prepares us for life's ups and downs, humbles and affirms us, roots us in where we are, and points us to where we're going.

Discovering Gospel-Shaped Liturgy

I came to appreciate liturgy during a time in our church's life when we were rediscovering the gospel. We planted the church in 2000, and for the first several years, we struggled to discern the best way to lead and unify the church.[6] Like many church leaders, we chased fads and searched for a "silver bullet" for ministry, something that nourished weary souls and called us to mission. By God's grace, the gospel broke through our thick skulls, and we came to see that the answer was not merely the ABCs of Christianity, but the A-to-Z of the Christian life. It was during this discovery that we began attempting to allow the gospel story to shape our gatherings. We wanted to structure the service in an arc based on the story of the gospel, rather than the emotional arc we'd cultivated up to that time. So we started moving the service through an intentional dialogue that remembered (directly and indirectly) the gospel.

---

[5] From a lecture at the Continuous Worship Conference, Mars Hill Church, Seattle, October 2007.
[6] I discuss this in a bit more detail in *Faithmapping*, which I cowrote with Daniel Montgomery.

122 RHYTHMS OF GRACE

We thought we were very clever and original, but all we were doing was rediscovering something that the church had been doing for a long time. In fact, most historical liturgies walk through the gospel story in one way or another. In *Christ-Centered Worship*, theologian Bryan Chapell spends some time reviewing the historic liturgies of a variety of liturgical and theological streams. "The common pattern of the order of worship in the church," he says, "reflects the pattern of the progress of the gospel in the heart."[7] These liturgies "re-present" the gospel and "reenact" the gospel.[8]

Chapell sees the pattern for this dialogue evidenced in the worship in the Scriptures, such as in Isaiah 6, Deuteronomy 5, 2 Chronicles 5–7, Romans 11–15, and Revelation 4–21.[9] (I would add the aforementioned Joshua 24 to this list as well.) The common sequence, which Chapell roots in the Scriptures and highlights in the various traditions, is this:

- adoration
- confession
- assurance
- thanksgiving
- petition
- instruction
- charge
- blessing[10]

The overarching movement is a retelling of the story, remembering that God is holy (adoration), we are sinners (confession and lament), Jesus saves us from our sins (assurance, thanksgiving, petition, and instruction), and Jesus sends us on his mission (charge and blessing). It's a movement that runs parallel to another way of thinking about the story of the gospel: creation, fall, redemption, and consummation (see fig. 1). In what follows, I want to explore the liturgy through that broad lens, looking at specific rhythms

---

[7] Chapell, *Christ-Centered Worship*, 99.
[8] Ibid., 99.
[9] Ibid., 103–11.
[10] Ibid., 100.

within the service, both from Chapell's list and from other biblical and historic practices.

Figure 1

Experiencing the Gospel	Remembering the Story	Actions in Liturgy
God is holy.	Creation	Adoration
We are sinners.	Fall	Confession (and/or) Lament
Jesus saves us.	Redemption	Assurance The Peace Prayers of Thanksgiving and Petition Instruction
Jesus sends us.	Consummation	Communion Commitment/Charge Blessing

There are many ways we can think about that overarching motif. Tim Keller identifies three general movements in the liturgy of John Calvin. During the Reformation in the 1600s, Calvin saw the need for a gospel-formed church that walked through deepening cycles of repentance when it gathered for worship. His liturgy followed three general movements: an Isaianic cycle (based on Isaiah 6: God reveals himself as holy, and we respond as sinners in need of mercy), a Mosaic cycle (the word is read and taught with the goal of seeing God's glory), and an Emmaus cycle (the church gathers around the table to see Jesus and responds in eating).[11] Keller's own liturgy uses the same general movement, with an adoration cycle, a renewal cycle, and a commitment cycle.[12]

Though the specific language might differ, a wide variety of traditions view gathered worship as a rehearsal of the gospel story. In this framework, worship is an invitation to step into the rhythms of grace. We remember our identity as gospel-formed

---

[11] Timothy J. Keller, "Reformed Worship in the Global City," in Carson, *Worship by the Book*, 217.
[12] Ibid., 226–35.

people, journeying together through the story that gave us our identity and being sent out to live gospel-shaped lives. Practiced in these rhythms, we learn to think in them, much as we learn to improvise on an instrument.

When learning improvisation, a musician most often begins by following note-for-note transcriptions of great improvisers. He might learn solos by Coltrane or Byrd, or study how Wes Montgomery comped through changes. After coming to some mastery of their decisions and styles, learning their licks and phrases, a student can begin incorporating them into his own playing, trying out a melodic line here or there, often unconsciously slipping their influence into his playing.

So it is with the grammar of grace. We submerge ourselves in it weekly, learning not merely through passive receptivity, but in very participatory ways. We stand and sit, sing and shout, lift our hands and bow our heads. We read the Scriptures aloud together, or listen as they're read aloud to us (which is a far different experience than reading them silently, as we're more prone to do). We welcome one another with handshakes and hugs, we hear the Word preached and proclaimed, we taste the bread and wine, and we send one another out with a blessing. Christian worship recognizes the fact that we're embodied creatures, engaging the whole person in the reenactment of the gospel story.[13]

Rehearsed regularly, the gospel becomes part of our way of thinking, seeing, feeling, loving, and being in the world. It's a weekly heartbeat, gathering us in and scattering us back out to our homes and workplaces, to children's soccer games and board meetings, to chemotherapy sessions and evenings around the dinner table. From there, we return to the gathered church, once again rehearsing the story, remembering who God has made us, singing and celebrating that identity. Liturgy that immerses the people of God in the rhythms of grace doesn't merely train them for gospel-centered worship; it trains them for gospel-centered lives.

---

[13] Smith, *Desiring the Kingdom*, 140–41.

So let's look at these rhythms in detail. In each section below, I'll identify the goals and purposes of each rhythm or movement in the liturgy and offer an example or two. In appendix B, you'll see a list of resources (many of which are available online) that can further help flesh out the various movements. One more preliminary note: while singing is particularly mentioned in specific places, it should be said that singing can also happen in any movement of the service.

God Is Holy—Creation

Call to Worship

Worship begins with God. It begins in the purity and perfection of his own being. It begins there because apart from his own creative action, there would be nothing else. It begins with him because he made light and dark, earth and sea, wide-stretching skies and deep-gouged valleys, and all of creation hums with energy and brilliance that God sums up in the understated word "good." The heavens declare his glory, not as a conscious act, but as a testimony in their very being to the ingenuity of their Maker. Worship begins with God because God begins everything, and everything that exists is a testimony to his handiwork. Worship begins with God because God made us in his image, a mysterious stamp that hard-wires us to reflect and declare his glory in a way that's unique among creation. In a sense, all his creative work is one big call to worship.

The first thing we need to acknowledge when we gather with God's church is that the whole thing—from the entire creation to the very thought of gathering to worship the Creator—was God's idea. We don't gather because we're clever. We don't meet because we've figured something out that the rest of the world has missed out on. We come because God is the great initiator. He made the world, he made us, and he is remaking us in Jesus. Our gatherings, our songs, our sermons, our fellowship around the table—all of it is a response to his initiation and invitation.

In one sense, worship can be thought of as a three-way conversation: God to us, us to God, us to one another. It can also be thought of as a vertical and horizontal conversation: vertical to God, horizontal to one another. But it's unquestionably a conversation that God initiates. When we gather and begin the conversation, we need to make it clear that God was the one who spoke first. This first movement acknowledges that God is holy and that he, our Creator, initiated all of the conversation that ensues.

One way we've framed that at Sojourn is by simply repeating the phrase, "God speaks, we respond." The whole point of the call to worship can be summed up in that phrase. God has spoken through creation, through his written Word, and through his Son. Everything we do is a response to his generous revelation of himself.

Getting Practical
- Historically, the call to worship is often a Scripture reading like Psalm 100:1–4.
- It can also be a great moment to invite the congregation to see their participation in the Trinitarian wonder of worship. A passage like Hebrews 8:1–6 or Philippians 2:1–11 can show how Jesus himself is our worship leader, and we invite the church to join us, by the power of God's present Spirit, as we join Jesus's songs and prayers before God's throne.

  - "The Holy Spirit, who is present here with us, invites us to join Jesus before the Father's throne as we sing and worship together."

- Don't be afraid to repeat certain simple phrases:

  - "Worship begins with God."
  - "God speaks, we respond."

Adoration and Praise
The dialogue then shifts to the church's response, which is typically songs and prayers of adoration. Adoration seems like a fairly innocuous activity—the least likely thing to be a point of conflict

in a conversation about worship. But adoration is also a declaration of war. God calls us to worship out of a world that's clamoring for us to worship a pantheon of idols. When the church hears God's call and begins to sing in response, it's simultaneously an affirmation of God's worth and a declaration of the worthlessness of the idols around us. John Witvliet explains:

> Every time we sing praise to the triune God, we are asserting our opposition to anything that would attempt to stand in God's place. Every hymn of praise is a little anti-idolatry campaign. . . . When we sing "Praise God, from whom all blessings flow," we are also saying "Down with the gods from whom no blessings flow."[14]

The goal of adoration is to put the character and glory of God on display in our songs and Scripture readings. Often, though, what passes for praise and adoration is actually songs about singing, or "worshiping worship" as it's been called. We sing about how great, loud, and enthused our worship is, all the while failing to declare much about the God who gathers us for worship.

While there's nothing wrong with singing about the actions of the church, the Psalms should always serve as a measuring stick for our celebration. Many psalms are declarations of love and devotion. And many psalms make reference to singing, dancing, and shouting. With that said, it should also be seen that the psalms rarely stay focused on that action and devotion, but return quickly to the God of Israel, who is worthy of such enthusiasm. Debra and Ron Rienstra, in *Worship Words*, remind us:

> We should note from the example of the Psalms that the lyric voice of the psalmist never stays focused on himself for long. The "I" of the Psalms always turns outward to consider the mighty deeds of God, God's faithfulness to God's people, and the way in which God's relationship with the speaker is surrounded by broader purposes for the world.[15]

---

[14] John D. Witvliet, "The Opening of Worship = Trinity," in Van Dyk, *A More Profound Alleluia*, 12.
[15] Rienstra and Rienstra, *Worship Words*, 52.

Songs of adoration and praise should not only be celebrative; they should also be descriptive. Whom are we praising? Why are we praising? As theologian Marva Dawn asks, "How will we sing to God a new song if we haven't learned anything about him, if we have not met him in this worship time, if he has not been the subject?"[16]

Remember: so we pray, so we believe. What kind of spirituality are we cultivating if we teach people that worship is fundamentally about their love, their song, their dance? What happens when life's storms hit and, like Israel in exile, we have no song left in us? Worship must fundamentally be about who God is and what he's done, not how great our singing, dancing, and loving is[17]—we're too prone to wander to be counted upon. But the song of Jesus continues with or without us, and the wonder of the gospel is the way it catches us up in it regardless of how we feel.

Bob Kauflin once asked a room full of worship leaders, "How long could you talk about God's glory? How much depth could you go into?" Our times of adoration and praise provide the language and images of God's glory for God's people. The words of Frederick Lehman quoted earlier bear repeating:

Could we with ink the ocean fill,
And were the skies of parchment made,
Were every stalk on earth a quill,
And every man a scribe by trade,
To write the love of God above,
Would drain the ocean dry.
Nor could the scroll contain the whole,
Though stretched from sky to sky.[18]

In praise and adoration, worship leaders serve like tour guides

---

[16] Dawn, *Reaching Out without Dumbing Down*, 109.
[17] Before you write me an angry e-mail about this, I'll acknowledge that there are worse songs than the one I'm thinking of here, and worse things that get said in praise music. I'll also acknowledge that it might be possible to take a song like this, introduce it with Scripture, and describe how God makes our love big and loud by his grace. But that's a lot of work to make that song have biblical weight and meaning, and I'm not entirely sure it's worth it.
[18] Frederick M. Lehman, "The Love of God," 1917.

to an inexhaustible wilderness, full of wonders and treasures that we can never fully explore. The challenge for us is to continually seek fresh language, fresh depths, fresh images to invite our congregations to sing and celebrate.

Getting Practical

- Take an inventory of the adoration and praise songs you sing in your church. Compare what they say to a list of the attributes of God (like those in Wayne Grudem's *Systematic Theology* or A. W. Pink's *Attributes of God*). What's missing? Are you leaning heavily on certain attributes over others?
- Ultimately, our emphasis in worship should be on who God is and what he's done. Along with the inventory above, consider whether your songs of praise are more about what we've done or what God has done.
- Praying prayers of praise is often difficult for people. We're very comfortable with thanksgiving prayers, but prayers of praise and adoration acknowledging and celebrating who God is can be much more difficult. Practice these by introducing your church to prose prayers, litanies, and psalms of praise that are spoken and read aloud during the service. (See appendix A for resources on this topic.)

We Are Sinners—The Fall

In Isaiah 6, the prophet beholds the glory of the Lord and immediately feels the intensity of his own fallenness. "Woe to me! For I am lost; for I am a man of unclean lips, and I dwell in the midst of a people of unclean lips; for my eyes have seen the King, the Lord of hosts!" (Isa. 6:5).

So it is with us. Our first response to God's revelation of himself is wonder and worship, and our next is the pain of our own uncleanliness. It's the story in Genesis 3. It's the plea of the crowd in Acts 2:37 when they cry out, "Brothers, what shall we do?" In worship, as in all of the Christian life, we need to cry out in our brokenness and hear the assuring comfort of our Savior. In the liturgy, this is the movement of confession and lament.

Confession

William Dyrness refers to this as a "healthy orientation to reality."[19]
As a community, our corporate confession of sin is a three-fold acknowledgment that (1) the world is not the way it was meant to be,
(2) we as a church are not the way we were meant to be, and (3) I
am not the way I was meant to be. Sin's invasion into our world
and our hearts has corrupted all of us, and apart from the mercy
of God, we are without hope.

Some pastors and worship leaders shy away from the habit of
confession because it feels so pointed. To ask the congregation (and
visitors) to acknowledge their sin can seem judgmental and hostile. It's better, they reason, to focus on the mercy and love of God.

I disagree. I actually have come to believe that confession of
sin is one of the most hospitable things we can do for both insiders (Christians) and outsiders (non-Christians). Most people are all
too well aware of their sin and their shortcomings and are busily
spinning their wheels in attempts to surmount them. They come
to our church gatherings and see happy people singing happy
songs about how their lives are all put together. They see Christians on television and in arenas promising health, wealth, and
happiness. The gritty brokenness of their own lives is discordant
with all this shiny veneer.

What if, instead, they came into a church gathering and heard:

Almighty God, we confess how hard it is to be your people.
You have called us to be the church,
    to continue the mission of Jesus Christ to our lonely and
        confused world.
Yet we acknowledge we are more apathetic than active,
    isolated than involved, callous than compassionate,
    obstinate than obedient, legalistic than loving.
Gracious Lord, have mercy upon us and forgive our sins.
Remove the obstacles preventing us
    from being your representatives to a broken world.

[19] William A. Dyrness, "Confession and Assurance = Sin and Grace," in Van Dyk, *A More Profound Alleluia,* 40.

Awaken our hearts to the promised gift of your indwelling
    Spirit.
This we pray in Jesus's powerful name. *Amen.*[20]

As Christians acknowledge their failures together, they testify
to the world that the plausibility of the gospel is rooted not in their
performance, but in the faithful mercy of God. Bryan Chapell says
it well: "Grace is all the more beautiful when we face the ugliness
of our sin. But we do not confess our wretchedness to wallow in
self-pity or merit divine mercy; we confess our destitution so that
our hearts will be enraptured anew and motivated afresh by the
riches of our Savior's love."[21] It doesn't have to be complicated. We
don't have to flagellate ourselves or eat ashes. As Dyrness says, it
simply means acknowledging reality.

Getting Practical

- There is no good news in the gospel without acknowledging
  the bad news of our sin. How are you communicating the bad
  news? How are you helping your congregation express the
  bad news?
- Confession can be sung as well as prayed. Consider singing
  through a setting of Psalm 51, or a song like "Give Us Clean
  Hands."
- Confession can be for corporate sins (how have we together
  failed to live out the gospel?) and individual sins (how have I
  personally failed to live out the gospel?).

Lament

Along with confession, we need to embrace the language of lament. The plague of sin has corrupted the world inside and out.
Just as we plead mercy for our individual and corporate brokenness, we lament the brokenness of the world around us. There's
no better model for this than the Psalms, which cry out again and
again, "How long, O Lord?"[22] They boldly ask God why he's absent,

---

[20] *The Worship Sourcebook*, 92.
[21] Chapell, *Christ-Centered Worship*, 183.
[22] See Psalms 13, 35, 79, 89, for instance.

why he's abandoned us, why he allows evil to run rampant, and when he'll come and crush his enemies once and for all.

These desperate cries are far removed from the standard fodder of much Christian culture. I often wonder what would happen if Joel Osteen (pastor of Lakewood Church in Houston and author of the positive-thinking best sellers *Your Best Life Now* and *Every Day a Friday*) walked onto the platform one Sunday and prayed through Psalm 88 with his church. The New Internation Version of the psalm ends with the hopeless whimper,

> You have taken my companions and loved ones from me;
> the darkness is my closest friend. (v. 18, NIV)

I imagine there'd be a stampede for the exits.

Funny as that thought may be, such a response would be common in many of our churches, regardless of their size and visibility. We live in a positive-thinking, high-achieving culture that celebrates victory, projects strength, and makes little room for personal weakness. When stories of weakness and tragedy do appear, they usually feature dramatic, happy endings (not unlike the show *Extreme Makeover: Home Edition*).

Triumph in this life is always partial and only temporary, whether in churches (consider the sad legacy of the Crystal Cathedral) or in the lives of individuals. Eventually, disease, age, or tragedy will catch us. We may be ninety or we may be twenty, but it will surely come. How are we preparing for that encounter?

What the church needs isn't empty promises of success in exchange for faith and tithing, but a gospel message that assures us that suffering is purposeful and that we have a God who is present in our suffering. When Matt Chandler, pastor of one of the fastest-growing churches of the last decade, was stricken with brain cancer, he faced it in a way that can only be described as otherworldly. I remember watching a video in which he was sharing about the suffering, talking about how much he longed to see his kids grow up and get married. Through tears he acknowledged both that God could take his life and that God is good—that being with Jesus would be better. In an interview with Justin Taylor, he said:

> There were at least three meetings with my doctors early on where I felt like I got punched in the soul. In those moments when I was discombobulated and things felt like they were spinning out of control, my theology and the Spirit were there to remind me that "he is good and he does good"—to remind me that God has a plan for his glory and my joy that he is working. I was reminded that this cancer wasn't punitive but somehow redemptive (Romans 8).[23]

Chandler's faith is both exemplary and ordinary. In a world where we cling to youth and wealth, where disease and death are hidden away and unwelcome in polite conversation, to hear him declare this confidence is profoundly countercultural. But it's also ordinary. It's the faith that was evidenced in countless Christians who were marched to their death in the Roman Empire, or who face death around the globe even now. It's the confidence of Henry Lyte, who, as he neared his own death, penned the words:

> I fear no foe, with Thee at hand to bless;
> Ills have no weight, and tears no bitterness.
> Where is death's sting? Where, grave, thy victory?
> I triumph still, if Thou abide with me.[24]

The gospel (and the gospel alone) can give someone that kind of confidence in the face of death. It frees us to bring the anxiety and pain of suffering before God, and there we find the hopeful presence we need to sustain us. Just as the psalmists cried out, we can cry out, lamenting the infection of sin that pervades our world, both for those who presently experience its weight and for those who inevitably will. Every Sunday, people walk through the doors of our churches facing similar challenges. They come with

---

[23] From Matt Chandler's interview with Justin Taylor, accessed http://thegospelcoalition.org/blogs/justintaylor/2010/11/01/one-year-later-an-interview-with-matt-chandler/.
[24] Henry Lyte, "Abide with Me," 1847.

AIDS and cancer. They come from homes with abusive spouses and rebellious children. They carry burdens of debt and joblessness, plagues of addiction and chronic pain, barren wombs and shattered dreams. In Israel and in the historic church, they could join in singing, "How long, O Lord?" How are we equipping them to sing in the desert? How are we preparing those who think they're immune?

For several years, on Mother's Day we've prayed a prayer of lament with those who long to be mothers but feel the pain of childlessness and loneliness. The section in italics is spoken as an introduction to the prayer:

> *We recognize on a day like today that everything in God's creation isn't as it should be. Sin has broken families and caused deep pain and heartache, and suffering in creation has led to suffering in the flesh—some who long to be parents are unable to experience that joy. Let's pray together, knowing that God hears us in our pain and sadness:*
>
> Lord, on this Mother's Day
> we lift up the aching hearts
> of all those who long to be mothers,
> but mourn the absence of new life within them;
> who have conceived,
> but suffered loss through miscarriage or abortion;
> who have given birth,
> but endured the tragedy of burying a child.
>
> Their grief is often hidden from us
> or neglected on this day of celebration of motherhood.
> We pray that they may experience healing in this church family.
>
> How long, O Lord, must death get its way at the outset of
>   new life?
> How long must joy be deferred or interrupted by such cruel
>   sorrow?
>
> Risen Lord of life, grant them comfort and peace,
> breathe in us all the breath of new life.
> Through Jesus Christ,

who defeated death,
Amen.[25]

Not only does such a prayer speak to specific and deep pain; it helps the congregation share the burden of that pain. Many on a day like Mother's Day are joyfully distracted by their own celebrations, and those who suffer do so in isolation. A prayer like this softens the hearts of those who are joyful, and embraces those who are cold.

Lament is important enough for the people of God that it was included in our songbook, the Psalms. It was important enough that God himself lamented from the cross (Matt. 27:46) and from the hills overlooking the brokenness of Jerusalem (John 11:35). Hebrews 5:8 tells us that Jesus "learned obedience through what he suffered," a fascinating statement. While we may never get to the bottom of the Trinitarian mystery that's glimpsed there, we can find comfort in knowing that God, in Jesus, has suffered like us and prays for us and with us with perfect compassion and understanding.

Getting Practical

- If lament is new for you and your congregation, start by praying through a psalm of lament (like Psalm 42 or 43).
- Give people space to process lament. Silence and space for reflection will help people connect their prayers with the places of sadness and loss in their own lives.
- One of the best times to practice lament is in the aftermath of significant tragedy. Local disasters like tornadoes, fires, or the death of a beloved church member or leader leave believers wrestling with God, and giving them words to voice that lament equips them to continue praying after the service.
- Lament is an ideal time to point to the priesthood of Jesus, reminding our churches that Jesus has suffered with and for us, and now compassionately prays for us in the midst of our suffering.

---

[25] Written by Nathan Bierma, printed with permission from the author.

136 RHYTHMS OF GRACE

Jesus Saves Us—Redemption

Words of Assurance

In the first movement of the liturgy, God reveals and we respond. In the second movement, we're still responding to his self-revelation, but this time with the pain of our own sinfulness. To this we hear God respond just as he responds to his people throughout Scripture when they cry out for mercy.

Like adoration, gospel-fueled assurance is a countercultural action. As James K. A. Smith points out, we live in a culture that constantly offers empty assurance. These "Oprah-fied secular liturgies tend to offer an illusory self-confidence ("Believe in yourself!") that refuses to recognize failure, guilt, or transgression."[26] It's assurance without confession, good news without any acknowledgment of the bad news. As the prophet Jeremiah said,

> They have healed the wound of my people lightly,
>   saying, "Peace, peace,"
>   when there is no peace. (Jer. 8:11)

The only voice that can offer true peace is the voice of God. David says in Psalm 51:4, "Against you, you only, have I sinned." If our sin has ultimately only offended God, then only his voice can offer the peace we need, and only after we've acknowledged reality.

In the liturgy, once sins are confessed, we hear an answer from the voice of God that assures us, "It is finished."

> Where is the god who can compare with you—
>   wiping the slate clean of guilt,
> Turning a blind eye, a deaf ear,
>   to the past sins of your purged and precious people?
> You don't nurse your anger and don't stay angry long,
>   for mercy is your specialty. That's what you love most.
> And compassion is on its way to us.
>   **You'll stamp out our wrongdoing.**
>   **You'll sink our sins**

---

[26] Smith, *Desiring the Kingdom*, 180.

to the bottom of the ocean.
You'll stay true to your word to Father Jacob
and continue the compassion you showed Grandfather
   Abraham—
Everything you promised our ancestors
from a long time ago. (Mic. 7:18–20, MESSAGE)

This is the word of the Lord: In Christ, your sins are forgiven.
Thanks be to God.

A passage like the one above might be read in response to confession, with the bold portions read together. It reinforces the dialogue of the gospel: as we cry out for mercy, God responds to us, reminding us that in Christ our sins are forgiven.

Similarly, in the wake of prayers of lament, we can look to God's promises of restoration. After laying out the painful effects of our broken world, we can hear the Word of God and the promise of restoration:

A day is coming when Jesus will return and set everything right and gather his family for eternity. Hear this hopeful vision the apostle John was given:

And I heard a loud voice from the throne saying, "Behold, the dwelling place of God is with man. He will dwell with them, and they will be his people, and God himself will be with them as their God. **He will wipe away every tear from their eyes, and death shall be no more, neither shall there be mourning, nor crying, nor pain anymore, for the former things have passed away."** (Rev. 21:3–5)
And he who was seated on the throne said, "Behold, I am making all things new."

Another way to offer assurance after lament is to communicate the contrast of present sorrow and future hope.

To all who suffer, the Lord says this:

So we do not lose heart. Though our outer self is wasting away, our inner self is being renewed day by day. For this light momentary affliction is preparing for us an eternal weight of glory beyond all comparison, as we look not to the things that are seen but to the things that are unseen. For the things that are seen are transient, but the things that are unseen are eternal. (2 Cor. 4:16–18)

Lord, open our eyes to see the hope of glory, and may that light outshine these momentary afflictions. We ask in Jesus's name, amen.

Getting Practical

- The words of assurance don't have to be lengthy. They're not the sermon. They're a simple reminder that God has heard us, and in Christ, he's forgiven us.
- Bryan Chapell points out that it's important to note where the forgiveness comes from.[27] We want to point the congregation to the God who forgives, and avoid giving the sense that we might be doing the mediating. "You're forgiven!" or the traditional "I grant you pardon" can give the false impression that the one speaking offers such pardon.

The Peace

Paul begins almost every one of his letters with a greeting of peace. It's not an arbitrary peace, and it's not a superficial peace. It's a peace that flows directly from "God our Father and the Lord Jesus Christ" (see Rom. 1:7; 1 Cor. 1:3; Gal. 1:3; Eph. 1:2; Phil. 1:2; 1 Thess. 1:1; 2 Thess. 1:2; 1 Tim. 1:2; 2 Tim. 1:2; Titus 1:4; Philem. 1:3; and more). This is a natural result of the gospel. When we stand together before God's judgment throne, recognizing what our sins deserve and what we've been graciously given in Jesus Christ, the walls of hostility between us crumble. We see that we have no right to hold a grudge or to stand in judgment over one another.

In almost all Christian worship traditions, there is some expression of that peace. In most contemporary churches, there's a time of greeting, when the members take a few moments to shake hands and welcome those around them. In liturgical practice, it's

---

[27] Chapell, *Christ-Centered Worship*, 196.

called "Passing the Peace," and it's often a formulaic handshake, with people uttering "Peace" to one another.

At the heart of this practice is the command given repeatedly in the New Testament to greet one another with a "holy kiss" (Rom. 16:16; 1 Cor. 16:20; 2 Cor. 13:12; 1 Thess. 5:26). While kissing strangers wouldn't go over well in most North American churches, the principle is clear: greet one another with affection. Welcome strangers. Share joy and peace when you come together.

Welcoming one another with love and peace flows naturally from the ongoing gospel dialogue in the service. We recognize that God is holy, we are sinners, and Jesus reconciles us to God *and* to one another. So we respond to that revelation by welcoming one another with peace, as family.

In practice, this might not look too different from an ordinary "greeting time" in a service, but in our hearts, it can be much deeper. It can be far more meaningful if we connect that hug, handshake, or high-five to the fact that, in Christ, there is no Jew or Greek, male or female, barbarian, Scythian, slave, or free, or (for that matter) black or white, Democrat or Republican, or rich or poor. All of our common cultural hostilities are dissolved by the mercy of Jesus. If we can make that clear as we lead worship, when the church turns to welcome one another, they will see each other with new eyes.

It can be as simple as saying:

> God has ended the hostility between him and us, and between us and one another. That means that because of the gospel, we have true peace with one another. We're a family—so let's welcome each other as a family.

It can also be led with a Scripture reading:

> *Hear the teaching of Christ:*

> A new command I give you,
> that you love one another as I have loved you.

The peace of Christ be with you all.
And also with you. (based on John 13:34)[28]

Getting Practical

- Greeting becomes routine very quickly. We need to regularly remind people of the reason for welcoming each other. Fresh language is very important here too.
- Help people imagine what it's like to be a stranger in the gathering. Ask them to put themselves in the other person's shoes and to love and welcome the strangers as they'd want to be welcomed.
- Give the greeting more time occasionally. Let people get lost in conversations with new people from time to time.

Giving/Offering

Giving, too, is something that flows directly from the gospel. In 2 Corinthians 8–9, Paul connects Christian generosity to Jesus's sacrificial example and calls believers to respond in kind, following the example of Christians who, despite their poverty, pleaded to give to the apostles' mission. The passage shows how New Testament giving is a worshipful response to the gospel: with transformed hearts, we're released from the idolatry of money and empowered to give it away.

Jesus spoke more about money than about heaven or hell. Eleven of thirty-nine parables are about money, and his teaching on money *always* connects it to the heart. The gospel that saves us motivates us, and should move us away from money idols and toward generosity, eager to support the mission of God, the pastors and shepherds of the church, and brothers and sisters in need. The offering during our weekly service is an opportunity to deconstruct one of the human heart's greatest idols. Every week, we can point to how Jesus shows us how to give and the gospel invites us to give.

More often than not, we treat giving like a chore or something we should apologize for asking worshipers to do. We attempt to

---

[28] *The Worship Sourcebook*, 125.

motivate giving with pictures of new buildings, number goals, and big thermometers, but in our churches' minds, it's just another consumer endeavor, another financial burden. The gospel tells us that giving is a privilege and to which we are invited, something we're *free* to do because we're no longer enslaved to money. So the call to give is a call to worship, and something we never need to apologize for or take for granted.

> *God's Word reminds us that giving is an act of worship when it calls giving a sacrifice:*
>
> Do not neglect to do good and to share what you have, for such sacrifices are pleasing to God. (Heb. 13:16)

Sometimes a simple prayer can make the whole picture clear as well.

> God has shown us the meaning of generosity in the beautiful
>   diversity of creation,
>   in the overflowing love of Jesus Christ,
>   in the never-ending gift of the Holy Spirit.
> God has abundantly blessed us and called us to be a
>   community that honors each other,
>   to serve others with joy,
>   to share our love and material possessions.
> Let us rejoice in what we have been given and in what is ours
>   to give.[29]

To be clear—I'm not saying that connecting giving to concrete needs is inappropriate, but the primary motivator for our giving (and our calls for sacrifice) should be the transforming power of the gospel.

> *We continue in our worship now as we give, remembering the words of Jesus:*
>
> For where your treasure is, there your heart will be also. (Matt. 6:21)

---

[29] Ibid., 238.

Getting Practical
- Giving is often rote, and worship leaders often apologize for the offering. Try instead to seize the opportunity to point out the ways in which it's a call to worship.
- Allow the Scriptures to make the hard call to give, pointing to the heart as the root of any lack of generosity.
- Be thankful: giving should always be asked for with a spirit of thankfulness on the part of pastors and worship leaders.

Pastoral Prayers

What's often called the pastoral prayer or the prayer of thanksgiving logically falls at this point in the service, after the church has acknowledged that God is holy, we are sinners, Jesus saves us, and Jesus reconciles us. As a community united by the gospel, we come together in prayer before God with thankfulness and prayer requests.

During the English Reformation, the pastoral prayer was a key motivating factor for the Free Church movement. Instead of reading prayers from a prayer book, followers of this movement believed that the prayer should be led by a pastor and should be geared directly to reflect the needs of the congregation. These prayers tended to be lengthy, theologically dense, and particular to the needs of the church. Pastors were encouraged to prepare well for them.[30]

If you've never seen copies of Spurgeon's pastoral prayers, you should try to hunt them down. They're enormous—longer than many sermons. They're rich with theology and pastoral wisdom, and they put to shame the casual, often flippant improvised prayers that we see in our worship services. Spurgeon knew that the pastoral prayer was a key moment in the service for modeling prayer to the congregation, as worthy of careful planning and preparation as any sermon.

Getting Practical
- If the pastoral prayer follows giving, it is good to acknowledge the offering in your thanksgiving prayer, and in your peti-

---

[30] R. Kent Hughes, "Free Church Worship: The Challenge of Freedom," in Carson, *Worship by the Book*, 145.

tions, as you ask God to bless those offerings and make them fruitful.

- Prayer, like all of worship, is always Trinitarian: offered by the power of the Spirit, through the mediation of the Son. We can acknowledge this in a variety of ways as we pray, and we should.

- Churches of various sizes will need to treat petitions differently. Some churches are of a size that could easily pray through the requests of the whole church. Some would need an entire day of prayer to accomplish such a list. It's worth wrestling with ways to name specific needs of the church in the gathering, just as we should acknowledge great needs that affect the broader community.

Instruction: The Sermon

What I say here might be the shortest discussion of preaching in print. That's because I'm far from an expert on preaching, and because anything I might say has been said with more authority and clarity by others.[31]

I will say this: in the context of a gospel-centered worship service, a sermon that opens the Scriptures and reveals Jesus is crucial. It's a microcosm of the gospel's centrality to all of life: the redeemed people of God remember the gospel, open the Scriptures, and hear again the gospel. We never move past that message. Preaching should always be an Emmaus road experience, wherein the Scriptures are opened and explained in such a way that Jesus is revealed as the key that holds the whole story together (see Luke 24:27; John 5:39).

Jesus Sends Us—Consummation

Worship in the local church (and the whole of the Christian life) exists between two worlds. We live in the light of the resurrection, but we live in a darkened world that awaits its fullest re-

---

[31] See Bryan Chapell, *Christ-Centered Preaching*; Edmund Clowney, *Preaching Christ in All of Scripture*; Timothy J. Keller and Edmond P. Clowney, "Preaching Christ in a Postmodern World," on iTunes: http://itunes.apple.com/us/itunes-u/preaching-christ-in-postmodern/id378879885.

newal in the return of Jesus and the restoration of all things. In the "already" of redemption and the "not yet" of consummation.

The Lord's Supper

No symbol quite captures this sense of timelessness like the Lord's Supper. We gather at a table whose roots stretch not only to the first century, but all the way back to the exodus. Jesus was feasting with his disciples on the Passover, a meal that God gave Israel to protect them from the plague of death and to forever remind them of his mercy. It's a meal that has continued in the church for two thousand years, and it's a foretaste of a meal that will be eaten in the New Jerusalem at the wedding feast of the Lamb. Past, present, and future come together at the table, connecting Israel's Passover to the body and blood of Jesus and offering a through-a-glass-darkly foretaste of the wedding feast of the Lamb. It's a beautiful, tangible, concrete gift where we can physically remember the gospel story.

The Lord's Supper was central to the worship of the early church,[32] and for much of history has been central to the weekly gathering of the church. During the Reformation, Martin Luther and John Calvin advocated weekly Communion, but Swiss Reformer Ulrich Zwingli opposed it, preferring a quarterly Communion celebration. For Zwingli, the Lord's Supper, when taken weekly, ran the risk of making the congregation superstitious or idolaters. (This view, of course, formed in the shadow of the Catholic Mass.) In most traditions since the Reformation, Zwingli's influence won out, and Communion is practiced far less regularly.

I tend to think that Zwingli's response was overreactive. If we are biblical when we serve Communion, we can make very clear that the Supper is a remembrance of the saving grace of God, and not a ritual that saves. If we are pastoral, then like singing, praying, and preaching, Communion can remain a fresh experience from week to week. As Robert Rayburn said, "I have never heard

---

[32] Chapell, *Christ-Centered Worship*, 291.

any Christian say, 'Let's be careful not to have our pastor preach the Word too often.'"[33]

At Sojourn, we practice Communion weekly. We serve it at the end of the sermon—allowing the preaching of Christ to transition naturally to feasting and celebrating Christ. We always read (or recite) the words of institution from 1 Corinthians 11:23–26:

> On the night when he was betrayed took bread, and when he had given thanks, he broke it, and said, "This is my body which is for you. Do this in remembrance of me." In the same way also he took the cup, after supper, saying, "This cup is the new covenant in my blood. Do this, as often as you drink it, in remembrance of me." For as often as you eat this bread and drink the cup, you proclaim the Lord's death until he comes.

As James K. A. Smith describes it, "It's as if the story we've been hearing and rehearsing now comes with live illustrations."[34] Smith goes on to point out that God gives us physical elements— bread and wine—to remind us that redemption isn't a merely spiritual or gnostic reality.[35] Instead, the physicality of bread and wine are a symbol and a foretaste of the redemption of all things.

At Sojourn, we also "fence the table"—making it clear that only those who have trusted in Christ for salvation are welcome at the table (see 1 Cor. 11:27). Those who haven't yet trusted Jesus are invited to a prayer room, where they can talk with a leader or a pastor.

Sojourn is just one example, and there are many good ways to serve this meal. One of my favorite examples is the Church of the Servant in Grand Rapids, Michigan, where Communion is served around a large table in the front of the worship space. The church forms a big circle around the table, and each member serves the bread and wine to the member next to him or her. As you might imagine, it takes a while. The circle isn't large enough to serve

---

[33] Ibid., 292.
[34] Smith, *Desiring God's Kingdom*, 198.
[35] Ibid., 198–99.

everyone at once, so it forms several times during the service as members serve one another and return to their seats, beautifully capturing the sense of a family meal.

I happen to love the historic confession that often precedes Communion in many Catholic and Anglican churches:

> Leader: Therefore we proclaim the mystery of our faith.
> Congregation: Christ has died! Christ is risen! Christ will
>   come again!

It's a declaration that recognizes the unique place of the church gathered around the table in a mysteriously tense moment wherein a single act remembers the past, embraces the present, and hopes for the future. At the heart of that declaration is the crucified Savior, who was slain before the foundations of the world and will be worshiped in glory for endless ages to come.

Getting Practical

- Each church's theology and ecclesiology will govern who is served Communion and how. It's good to consider how you might indicate the familial nature of the meal. Often this is done by using a single cup or by pulling all of the elements (if they're to be distributed) from a single table.
- Because it's a meal with multiple layers of meaning, it can be practiced and celebrated a variety of ways. It can be a somber meal, eaten on the eve of Christ's death. It can be a celebration of our exodus from darkness to light. It can be a foretaste of the wedding supper. You don't have to cover all the bases every week.

Commitment/Preparation for Sending

There's a sense in which the Lord's Supper, with its eye to the future, turns our attention to the mission. The day is coming when Christ will return to judge the living and the dead, and the urgency of that day's approach calls us to go back into the world serious about mission and serious about living out the new identity given to us as God's people. An affirmation of faith or an affirmation of commitment is sometimes confessed together before the church is sent out.

One way to do this is in connection with the sermon. A historical confession, a catechism question, or a Scripture reading can prepare the congregation to be sent out with deepened clarity about who God has made them and where he's calling them. One example might be this reading (and the introduction to it):

> *Today, we've opened God's Word and seen the supremacy of Jesus, our Mediator. Let's make this declaration, together with saints who've affirmed it for hundreds of years:*
>
> **Jesus Christ only is made the Mediator of the new Covenant, even the everlasting Covenant of grace between God and Man, to be perfectly and fully the Prophet, Priest and King of the Church of God for evermore.** (The Tenth Declaration of the London Baptist Confession)

It's also helpful to reinforce the message with songs that recapitulate what was taught, or that call the church out into the world. Matt Redman's "Mission's Flame" is a great contemporary example of a song that does this, as is "Oh Church Arise," by Keith Getty and Stuart Townend.

Getting Practical

- In the aftermath of the sermon, it's good to ask the congregation to repeat and reaffirm what was taught.
- I love using historic resources for the commitment (see appendix A) because doing so connects our service and teaching with the historic church. In other words, it reminds folks that we didn't make this stuff up.
- A hopeful turn happens as we look to the future return of Christ, when (as Tolkien has said) "all the sad things will come untrue."

Benediction

The service ends with a benediction, which is a sending blessing. "A blessing for the road" as we've called it at Sojourn for years.

Chapell reminds us that it's "not simply a Scripture verse with a nice sentiment or a summary of the Sermon's message." It's "sending God's people out with the promise of divine pardon, presence, and peace."[36]

Worship services that end with a casual "Y'all come back next week" miss the chance to remind members of the body of Christ that they aren't simply leaving: they're being sent. I love James K. A. Smith's description of the benediction:

> Worship, like creation, ends as it began: with God's blessing. . . . When we were called, we were blessed; now as we're sent, we're blessed. We are not sent out as orphans, nor are we sent out to prove ourselves. The blessing speaks of affirmation and conferral—that we go empowered for this mission, graced recipients of good gifts, filled with the Spirit, our imaginations fueled by the Word to imagine the world otherwise.[37]

The benediction has a centrifugal force to it[38]—spinning us out from the gathering to our scattered lives where worship continues as before, but in our varied corners. Historically, the benediction is almost always Trinitarian, and in this way it reminds us that we scatter in the same mysterious Trinitarian dance in which we gather. Here are a couple of historic examples:

> "The peace of God, which passeth all understanding, keep your hearts and minds in the knowledge and love of God, and of His Son, Jesus Christ our Lord. And the blessing of God Almighty, the Father, the Son, and the Holy Spirit be amongst you, and remain with you always." Amen.[39]

> May the grace of Christ our Savior,
> And the Father's boundless love,
> With the Holy Spirit's favor,
> Rest upon [you] from above.

---

[36] Chapell, *Christ-Centered Worship*, 254.
[37] Smith, *Desiring God's Kingdom*, 207.
[38] I got this concept from David L. Stubbs's discussion of blessing in "Ending of Worship = Ethics," in Van Dyk, *A More Profound Alleluia*.
[39] Blunt, *The Annotated Book of Common Prayer*, 396.

Thus may we abide in union,
With each other and the Lord,
And possess, in sweet communion,
Joys which earth cannot afford.[40]

And a great scriptural example:

> The grace of the Lord Jesus Christ and the love of God and the fellowship of the Holy Spirit be with you all. (2 Cor. 13:14)

Getting Practical

- The call to worship and the benediction are like bookends to the service. Consider connecting the two in some way.
- In many traditions, the pastor extends his hands to offer the blessing. Sometimes the congregation extends theirs to receive it as well.
- Like the assurance, we want to make very clear that the blessing is offered by God, not by us. (This is why some prefer scriptural benedictions.)

The Goal of the Liturgy

Taken together, these rhythms help the church pray and sing through a full range of human experience. The gathering isn't simply a single spiritual discipline; it's a host of them. It's a way of taking the experiences of prayer and worship, which we so often compartmentalize and individualize, and unifying them in the life of the congregation. They're Word-centered habits, too. It's easy (and, frankly, a good idea) to allow Scripture to be the primary thing spoken and read through the various prayers and songs in the service. As Paul says in Colossians 3:16 and Ephesians 5:18–20, as we sing, pray, read, and preach God's Word together, he dwells among us richly in the Spirit.

The Spirit's work will enable us to carry all of these habits with us as we go. The way we adore, confess, and lament together will shape the way we adore, confess, and lament in our ordi-

---

[40]John Newton, "May the Grace of Christ Our Savior," *Olney Hymns*, 329.

nary lives. When people spend months or years praying psalms of lament, they're better prepared to face the day that tragedy strikes, as the Spirit of God brings these words and prayers to mind. When they learn every week to extend grace and peace to friends and strangers in the gathering, it helps them to do so in the rest of life. As they face and voice their sinfulness and learn to express it together, they will more easily face and voice their sinfulness in their scattered lives.

The gathering shapes our ordinary life, and ordinary life shapes our experience of the gathering. Our burdens and guilt, joys and celebrations inevitably come with us. We gather not to escape these burdens and joys, but to bring them to a place where we acknowledge what is most true, most real, and most valuable. There, in the light of the gospel, all of these emotions and all of the circumstances of our lives are revealed in their proper place, and God speaks a word of peace over them.

So we hold them up as we celebrate and thank, we hold them up as we confess and lament, and in return, we hear the voice of God, thundering from his Word and his Son, pouring out grace upon grace as we remember, recommit, and are sent again into the world.

Chapter 9

SING, SING, SING

I recently found myself boiling with frustration. I was at one of those church conferences where the stage was populated by church innovators, and I was especially troubled by one in particular, a man with many published books and a packed schedule of speaking engagements at churches, conferences, seminaries, and colleges around the globe. He writes and speaks about the future of the church, primarily advocating small "missional" house churches.

"Imagine yourself sitting in a coffee shop," he said, "and the person at the table next to you pulls out an acoustic guitar and starts singing praise songs." He almost spat as he said the words "praise songs." "I mean seriously," he continued, "we invite unbelievers into our church lives, and suddenly we force them into environments where they're surrounded by people singing and weeping, raising their hands, doing all kinds of weird things that you never, ever see in the other areas of their lives. It's bizarre."

For him, the answer was to make church look more like the coffee shop: conversational and communal. Gather in a home, share a meal, open the Word, and let it speak. But don't sing. That just alienates people.

This all sounds reasonable enough until you open the Bible and read the word "sing." And then you read it again—and again. And you see references to singing as the patriarchs do it, as the tribes of Israel do it, as the church does it, and ultimately as the body of saints gathered in the New Jerusalem do it. God himself sings in Zephaniah 3:17, and as Reggie Kidd argues, when the church sings, we join the song that Jesus sings as he stands before the Father and leads us in worship.[1]

Our faith is a sung faith. The people of God sing in war and peace, victory and defeat, celebration and lament. On the one hand, our singing *is* otherworldly. We sing an ancient song that climaxes in the hazy but hope-filled future. We sing as living people among the walking dead.

On the other hand, the speaker's idea that people don't sing anymore is just plain wrong. Go to a Pearl Jam concert (or to You-Tube) and watch what happens when Eddie Vedder begins to sing "Betterman." Go see U2 and listen as the crowd takes over songs like "I Still Haven't Found What I'm Looking For." Go to a soccer game in Europe, and listen as proud fans bellow their team's anthems after a scored goal. (For that matter, go to a busy pub in the UK and witness the same.)

We sing to babies and we sing with our kids. We listen to music day and night, like it's a soundtrack to our lives as it pours from our computers, iPhones, and MP3 players.

The Challenge of Music

Debate over music is nothing new. In the years after the Reformation, there were debates about the use of instruments, about singing songs that weren't psalms, and about musical style. When we were planting Sojourn in 1999–2000, several core members rose up and argued that we should only sing hymns. Mind you, this was in an urban church plant, and these folks were eighteen to twenty years old, some of whom played guitars and drums in worship ministries with me for years prior.

For many of us, our music-related preferences are as heated an issue as politics. We love what we love, and we think everyone who disagrees with us is ignorant. When young folks show up and attempt to introduce new sounds and ideas, we feel embittered. Likewise, when we're dropped into an environment with

---

[1] Kidd, *With One Voice*, 21.

music from our grandparents' generation, we resort to sighing, yawning, and eye-rolling.

Today, when many worship services are reduced to preaching and music, it becomes very easy to equate music with worship—and that's a dangerous slope to park your car on. If music *is* worship, then when you mess with someone's musical preferences, you threaten their access to God. No wonder the debates become so heated.

I've deliberately waited until this late chapter to begin talking in detail about music and singing. I hope that by doing so, I've made it clear that the Bible's definition of worship (and for that matter, the church's definition for the larger part of its history) isn't exclusively music. Instead, worship in the gathered church is the total work of the people—the gathering of the church for prayer, preaching, sacred symbols (baptism and Communion), giving, and singing. I hope such a perspective can help us hold our musical preferences a little more loosely as we see them fitting into a larger purpose.

We also need to broaden our understanding of the role music plays. Because we tend to define worship as singing, we tend also to treat singing as an individualized encounter with God. So we go to church and sing with closed eyes while trying to avoid being distracted by the people around us. This too misses an important point. Worship is a broader thing than music, and music's purpose in the church is bigger than my personal experience. It's not merely *my* song, but *our* song. We sing together, uniting our voices and our words.

Word and Song: Colossians 3

Knowing that worship is more than music, we need to clarify what role music plays in our gatherings—how we're to engage it, what types of songs we should sing, and what our hearts' attitude should be toward it. To do so, I want to look primarily at Colossians 3:16, one of the places where Paul gives us an explicit instruction to sing and a description of what happens when we do. Here's the verse with a bit of its context:

> Here there is no Gentile or Jew, circumcised or uncircumcised, barbarian, Scythian, slave or free, but Christ is all, and is in all.
>
> Therefore, as God's chosen people, holy and dearly loved, clothe yourselves with compassion, kindness, humility, gentleness and patience. Bear with each other and forgive one another if any of you has a grievance against someone. Forgive as the Lord forgave you. And over all these virtues put on love, which binds them all together in perfect unity.
>
> Let the peace of Christ rule in your hearts, since as members of one body you were called to peace. And be thankful. Let the message of Christ dwell among you richly as you teach and admonish one another with all wisdom through psalms, hymns, and songs from the Spirit, singing to God with gratitude in your hearts. And whatever you do, whether in word or deed, do it all in the name of the Lord Jesus, giving thanks to God the Father through him. (Col. 3:11–17, NIV)[2]

The Community and Unity of Colossians 3:11–15

In the passage, Paul is painting a picture of a church marked by forgiveness and reconciliation. The gospel removes our ethnic and social barriers, and a unique unity emerges, birthed from the new hearts of God's people. So before we talk about what role music plays in the church, we have to see it in the light of the transforming power of the gospel. Paul presumes gospel-formed unity before he talks about singing.

In other words, the gospel should be what connects people— not music. Our differences are never so slight as they are at the foot of the cross. It's the ground upon which the church gathers, a place where social, political, ethnic, and cultural boundaries are obliterated, and instead, Christ is all and is in all. In that place we find peace, and that peace should be accompanied by a spirit of thanksgiving and unity. And in response, we sing.

---

[2] I'm using the NIV for this passage because I believe it makes the meaning of v. 16 most clear and explicit.

Somehow we've ended up in a place where the exact opposite is true. While Paul tells the Colossians that social and ethnic boundaries are obliterated for Christians, we have found ways to divide into new tribes based on musical preference: traditional and contemporary, classic and modern, hymns and praise choruses. My friend Chip Stam, referencing Harold Best, once said, "A mature Christian is easily edified."[3] If we're gathering humbly, united by the gospel, we should be marked by a sense of thankfulness that brings us together, regardless of our stylistic and cultural decisions.

The great tragedy of worship wars—of churches splitting and blasting each other over stylistic choices and song choices—is that it totally misses the reason we sing. The last thing we should do is sing "A Mighty Fortress Is Our God" with a scowl on our faces and resentment in our hearts toward our brothers and sisters across town who are singing "Mighty to Save" (and vice versa).

The reconciling work of the gospel is the prerequisite to our singing, just as it is the prerequisite to all of our worship. It's in the light of the gospel that we live, and everything—our living, breathing, singing, preaching, praying, working, parenting, and whatever else we do—should flow from thankful gospel-reconciled hearts.

The Word and Singing: Colossians 3:16[4]

Verse 16 is where we're going to camp out for a while. The verse is basically a command—"Let the message of Christ dwell among you richly"—followed by a description of the means to make that your reality: "as you teach and admonish one another with all wisdom through psalms, hymns, and songs from the Spirit, singing to God with gratitude in your hearts."

Here, Paul says that *the way the Word dwells richly among us* is by our teaching and admonishing one another with songs, hymns, and

---

[3] Taylor, "Easily Edified" (blog post).
[4] In *The New Worship* by Barry Liesch, there is an excellent appendix dealing with the debates around the passage. Liesch argues convincingly for the "instrumental view," which is what I articulate here. See also David Peterson, *Engaging with God*, 197–98, and 222n7.

spiritual songs.[5] In this view, the whole verse is a single command. To put it another way, we sing so that we can teach and admonish one another, resulting in the rich indwelling of God's Word in God's people.

If music in the church is just about consumeristic preference, then my singing is motivated by my personal tastes. If singing is about letting God's Word dwell among us, then my singing is motivated by love for God (whose Word I want dwelling with me) and love for my church family, whom I have the chance to admonish and encourage as I sing. If we believe that the Word of Christ dwells richly in us *as we sing it*, then the way we sing and what we sing have a much different importance. We don't want to miss out on the opportunity to experience the richness of God's indwelling Word, and we will if we treat song as something sentimental or optional.

Singing to One Another

As we saw in Chapter 5, the songs we sing have more than one audience. Colossians 3:16 says that we're teaching and admonishing one another as we sing. So our songs aren't meant "only for God." We're singing to "one another" too. We can glorify God as we testify to one another about who he is and what he's done. We can also encourage and build up one another as we sing praises to God, confess our sins, and lament the state of the world around us. Both a vertical and horizontal dynamic are present in the passage and throughout biblical examples of song. Here again, we have another motivation for singing: we sing to teach and admonish others in the church.

I remember one Sunday gathering when I came struggling with guilt. I sat in the back, brooding, feeling weak and unable to sing out. A stranger sat next to me, and during the services, we began singing "How Deep the Father's Love for Us." As we sang, my unknown companion belted out these lines:

---

[5] It's worth mentioning that there are a variety of views about what exactly Paul is saying in this verse. It's one of those verses where the placement of words and punctuation in the translation results in very different meanings.

It was my sin that held him there until it was accomplished;
His dying breath has brought me life—I know that it is
   finished.[6]

Now, someone could have sat me down and reminded me that my sin was paid for, and that might have spoken to me just as deeply—we'll never know for sure. But in that moment, it wasn't the words on the page but the testimony of the voice next to me that spoke to my soul. (And it wasn't a great voice either!)

Our singing is a testimony, a declaration to those around us of who we are and whose we are. Harold Best says, "A congregation is just as responsible to sing the gospel as the preachers are to preach it. These two tasks (singing and preaching) jointly undertaken to their fullest, then reduce themselves to one common act."[7] It's an expression of unity for us to join in one voice and declare to one another that we're on the same page. We're united around the same things. One gospel, one church, one faith, one voice, one song.

Singing in the Bible and Church History

Not only do we unite with the body of Christ in the church today; we unite with the people of God throughout history. Consider this:

- The Bible includes a songbook. I cringe when I hear the Psalms referred to as the great "prayer" book of the Bible—not because those chapters lack in their ability to guide us in prayer, but because first and foremost, the Psalms are songs.
- The command to sing occurs more than a hundred times in the Psalms, and many more times beyond that book.
- Genesis 4:21 takes time to mention the invention of musical instruments—we don't get to know who made the wheel, but we know who invented the harp and flute.
- Musicians were an integral part of the life of Israel—in the temple, in the kings court, and even in the armies, on one occasion leading the troops into battle singing, "Give thanks to the LORD, / for his steadfast love endures forever" (2 Chron. 20:21).

---

[6] Stuart Townend, "How Deep the Father's Love for Us," copyright © 1995 Thankyou Music.
[7] Best, *Music through the Eyes of Faith*, 192.

- Throughout history, revival has been accompanied by song-writing movements. This is true from the monastic renewals in the Middle Ages to the English Reformation and the Great Awakening in America.
- God himself sings! "He will rejoice over you with singing" (Zeph. 3:17).
- Jesus, as he breathes his last on the cross, cries out the first line from Psalm 22, a messianic psalm that shows our Savior suffering, then rising victoriously to lead an assembly in worship (Psalm 22; see also Heb. 2:12; 8:1–2).
- When we read of eternity, we find the people of God singing (Rev. 7:9–11).

The Bible gets much thinner if we take out all the songs and references to singing.

Why We Sing

So we have these lights to cast onto our singing: First and foremost, our singing should flow naturally from hearts that are grateful for the peace and reconciliation purchased for us in the gospel (Col. 3:11–15). Second, singing is a means God has chosen to allow the Word of Christ to dwell richly in us (v. 16). Third, we have a multitude of commands in the Scriptures to sing. Fourth, we have the examples of Israel, saints throughout church history, God the Father, and Jesus, our singing Savior.[8] Taken together, it's a compelling case that singing is a vital part of the Christian life.

With these before us, how can we justify entering a place of worship and letting out lackluster, under-our-breath singing? How can we justify a refusal to participate because "we don't like the songs"? The Bible doesn't call us to sing any less than it calls us to pray or read the Scriptures—and there's no escape clause if we don't like country music. Singing is a rich part of living out our faith, one of the means God has given us to experience the richness of his Word.

---

[8] This phrase comes from Reggie Kidd's excellent book, With One Voice. See, for instance, chap. 7.

What Do We Sing?

So then, what do we sing? In Colossians 3:16, Paul tells us to sing "psalms, hymns, and songs from the Spirit" (niv) or "spiritual songs" (niv84, esv, and many others). Here too, there is some debate and discussion regarding what exactly is meant by each of these words. It seems that throughout the New Testament the words for psalms and hymns are used interchangeably, and I've yet to find anyone with an authoritative interpretation of what is meant by "spiritual songs" (though there are plenty of interesting interpretations on the Internet!).

What seems to make the most sense is that Paul is referring to broad categories that would have been familiar to the Colossians. This church was likely a mixed audience of Jews and Gentiles, Romans and non-Romans. At the time this letter was written, there was already a body of hymns emerging and being passed around the various churches. Colossians 1:15–20 and Philippians 2:5–11, for instance, were early examples of hymns. The Psalms were integral to Jewish worship (in which the church's founders would have had a long history), and the New Testament writers quote from them regularly, so they too would likely have been a part of the life of the young church. It seems that when Paul uses the words "psalms" and "hymns," he is referring broadly to both the book of Psalms and the variety of other songs being written and sung among the churches.

As for "spiritual songs," the term could mean several things. It could mean songs inspired in the moment by the Holy Spirit—spontaneous, sung testimony. Some suggest it could be songs sung in tongues, but that isn't a very natural reading of the text. Others have said that perhaps "spiritual" is a modifier that could apply to all of the words—singing spiritual psalms, hymns, and songs. Still others suggest simply that "spiritual songs" refers to the continued emergence of new songs in the church.

Whatever the case, the passage as a whole tells us at least one thing clearly: singing in the church should be diverse. With the

Psalms as a guide and a standard, we can express an incredible range of emotions. I believe that the wording of Colossians 3 calls us to embrace diversity in the Psalms—referring to the biblical psalms, hymns (the two-thousand-year-old heritage of the songs of the church), and spiritual songs as the continued testimony of believers in new songs.[9]

Diversity is more of a challenge than it sounds. The range of psalms is much broader than the kinds of expression we're used to in the church. We don't sing a whole lot of songs asking God to crush his enemies. We probably don't often have the boldness to speak to God the way the psalmist does when he says,

> How long, O LORD? Will you forget me forever?
> How long will you hide your face from me? (Ps. 13:1)

There's a pretty big gap experientially between this sense of lament and the over-the-top happiness of much contemporary Christian music. It's not that joy is uncalled for—the Psalms have plenty of it! But the Christian life is a journey with both peaks and valleys.

Recognizing this is one of the gifts that the Psalms and that psalmic language give us. The historic hymns do this as well. Anne Steele wrote these beautiful words around 1760:

> Dear refuge of my weary soul,
> On thee when sorrows rise;
> On thee, when waves of trouble roll,
> My fainting hope relies.
>
> While hope revives, though pressed with fears,
> And I can say, "My God,"
> Beneath thy feet I spread my cares,
> And pour my woes abroad.
>
> To thee I tell each rising grief,
> For thou alone canst heal;

---

[9] I think we can also be open to the possibility of spontaneous, Spirit-filled song in much the same way as we can be open to any gift of the Spirit.

Thy word can bring a sweet relief,
For every pain I feel.

But oh! when gloomy doubts prevail
I fear to call thee mine;
The springs of comfort seem to fail
And all my hopes decline.

Yet gracious God, where shall I flee?
Thou art my only trust;
And still my soul would cleave to thee,
Though prostrate in the dust.[10]

Where today we shy away from lament and repentance in our songs, hymnals have devoted entire sections. Their authors knew the formative power of singing and that these words would be utterly necessary in the lives of their congregations in days when "sorrows rise" and "gloomy doubts prevail."

For a few years now, we've sung a song at Sojourn called "Absent from Flesh." It's an adaptation of a text from Isaac Watts, penned by a Sojourn elder and worship leader, Jamie Barnes. The song talks about the hope of the future, when our sin-stained bodies will be replaced with something more glorious. "This failing body I now resign, and the angels point my way," says the chorus.[11]

Late one night, I got a text from a close friend. His mother had been sick off and on for many years, and her health suddenly took a severe turn.

"My mother resigned her failing body tonight," he said. He went on to express his confidence and comfort in knowing that she was a Christian, and that she was now with Jesus.

I was struck on multiple levels. First, my friend's loss was a surprise, and though his mother had been sick, we weren't ex-

---

[10] Steele, *Poems on Subjects Chiefly Devotional*, 144.
[11] I'm often challenged, about this text, "Isn't that kind of gnostic?" I would argue that the text is using poetic language to describe the transcendent beauty of future hope. I would also argue that those who worry about this kind of language about bodies are often those who have never suffered physically with long-term pain or illness. For those who have suffered, the text makes perfect sense.

pecting her to pass so quickly. Second, I was moved that in that moment, the words of Watts's hymn were there with him, helping provide language and hope for his tragedy.

I've seen it again and again in our church, especially during personal testimonies during baptism services—lines from hymns sneaking their way into people's stories. That's what songs and hymns are meant to do. They provide language for experiences that often leave us speechless. They prepare us, as John Witvliet says, for our encounter with death.

> One wise pastoral musician said that every week as she led congregational singing, she was rehearsing the congregation for a future funeral. (This makes me wonder, What if we planned our music with this as a primary goal? "Musician, why did you choose that piece of music?" "Well, it fit the texts of the day, it was well crafted, it challenged us musically—but mostly I picked it because you'll need to know that piece when your family is preparing to bury a loved one.")[12]

Likewise, psalms and hymns orient us toward giving thanks in life's good seasons. The Doxology, sung in almost every English-speaking tradition, is a way to respond to almost every good thing that comes in life.

> Praise God, from Whom all blessings flow;
> Praise Him, all creatures here below;
> Praise Him above, ye heavenly host;
> Praise Father, Son, and Holy Ghost.[13]

Life isn't without its good gifts, and our songs of praise and thanksgiving teach us how to respond to them.

Biblical singing expresses a wide range of moods and emotions. Living in an already and not-yet reality, we experience the joys of forgiveness, the beauty and glory of the gospel, and reconciliation between God and one another; but we also live in a world

---

[12] Witvliet, *Worship Seeking Understanding*, 235.
[13] From the hymn, "Awake My Soul and with the Sun"; words by Thomas Ken, 1674.

still plagued with sin. We still suffer and struggle with what the Bible calls our flesh, and we eagerly await the day when Jesus will return again and make all things right. And we need help giving voice to that experience.

Singing with Grace

Colossians 3:16 ends with the words, "Singing with thankfulness in your hearts to God." Here again, the way we translate determines much about the way we understand the words. Barry Liesch, citing theologian Gordon Fee, points out that the word translated "gratitude" (or "thankfulness" in many translations) is never translated as "thankfulness" elsewhere in the New Testament. Instead, it's typically rendered as "the grace" or "in the grace." Liesch likes the New King James Version for the way it brings this out: "Teaching and admonishing one another in psalms and hymns and spiritual songs, singing with grace in your hearts to the Lord."[14]

Fee says, "The focus is not so much on our attitude toward God as we sing, but on our awareness of his attitude toward us." In other words, we sing to God with an awareness of his gracious action in our lives, and, Fee adds, it's "our standing in grace that makes such singing come from the heart."[15]

Taken together, the entire discussion of singing in Colossians 3 has grace as its bookends. Grace motivates us to sing, and when we sing, we are to sing with grace. We've been taught in our churches and in the Christian marketing subculture around us to treat music as another product for us to consume—just as we have the rest of our faith. If something doesn't meet our preferences, we've learned to discard it, join another church, and buy a different CD. We've learned to be spectators on Sundays—listening, enjoying, and critiquing—but the Bible unapologetically calls us to be participants.

---

[14] Liesch, *The New Worship*, 48.
[15] Gordon Fee, as quoted in ibid.

Singing and Modern Music

Singing can be challenging in our contemporary churches. A common criticism is that contemporary music is too hard to sing. The melodies, inspired by pop songs, are too wide-ranging, too syncopated, and too complex for a congregation of multiple voices to join in together. Let me offer three responses.

The first is agreement. Many contemporary Christian songs are far too complex for a congregation to sing together. Often songwriters put very little thought into the range of a tune or how easy it is to follow because songwriting is seen as a form of self-expression.

But songwriting for the church is a completely different task than songwriting as a performing artist. In the church, music should always be the servant of the congregation's singing. Colossians 3:16 makes that clear. We gather in order to sing to one another, and if the band's accompaniment or the stylistic choices inhibit participation, then we've failed. When this happens, music is no longer the servant of the church's worship, but the church is the servant of the music.

The Bono Principle for Corporate Worship

But that's not *always* the case with modern music, which brings me to my second response, which I like to call the Bono Principle for Corporate Worship. Here's how you put this to the test:

- Find a friend who is both a terrible singer and a U2 fan.
- Buy this friend (and yourself) a ticket to see U2.
- Watch to see if he sings along to "Where the Streets Have No Name," "Beautiful Day," or "Sunday Bloody Sunday."

Did the complexity of the song hinder singing along? What about the song's range? Or the loudness of the band?

The fact is that we will all sing with passion and energy if we're in a situation we find compelling and inspiring. This is particularly true if we're emotionally attached to the songs we sing.

U2 has a distinct advantage in these situations, of course. For their fans, their music is a soundtrack to life. We hear it on iPods, computers, and car stereos. The repeated experience of listening and singing along prepares the fan for the concert. He shows up ready to sing.

Digital Hymnals

A generation or two ago, there was a much wider degree of musical literacy, and the hymnal, with its printed melodies, helped the church to sing along with passion. Today, not only is that literacy eroded, but the hymnals are gone in many places too. Some churches seek to maintain that kind of musical visibility and literacy by printing large bulletins with all the music enclosed, but that solves only half the problem. The congregation is still, by and large, unable to read the music.

This brings me to the third point about contemporary songs: modern technology provides new avenues for preparing people to sing. This is one of the big reasons we began recording at Sojourn Music. We wanted to put the songs that were being written within the church in the hands of the congregation in a way that helped people to sing. On our website now, we have our "digital hymnal," a resource where we make simple arrangements of our songs available to those who want to learn the melodies, and we try to communicate in advance each week about what we're singing so that church members can come prepared. It's remarkable to hear the way a large group, after listening to a CD for a few months, is capable of singing together.

Not every church has the resources to record, but in the Internet age, there's no excuse for not equipping our churches with songs. Consider starting a blog or using a Facebook page to provide links on Amazon music or iTunes to the songs you're going to sing. Encourage your church members to spend twenty to thirty dollars on downloads of specific songs, loading them onto an iTunes playlist that they could listen to regularly in order to be prepared for Sundays. That kind of immersion can really transform the way the church participates.

One final thought on this critique of singing and modern music. We need to remember that the hymn tradition, with its strict melodies and unity of voice, is but one stream of congregational song. There are other cultural traditions and other ways of participating in singing with the church. In gospel music, for instance, each individual voice has more freedom, and different members of the congregation freely improvise in a beautiful polyphony. In some streams of church music, participation takes more of a call-and-response rhythm. I wonder if, for instance, hip-hop couldn't be employed in service of congregational worship in such a way.

The Goal of All Music: Helping People to Sing

The goal of music in the gathering isn't great sound or elaborate musicianship. It's a church gathered and united in song. Many who lament the advent of the rock ensemble in the local church point to the loss of beautiful a cappella singing. We have replaced it with the pervasive, quasi-Britpop sounds of contemporary praise. It's a good critique. When it comes to instruments and sound, more is not always better. Miles Davis is supposed to have said that the most important notes are the ones you don't play. Worship leaders need to work hard to minimize at times, to pull the band out of a song. Church musicians who know how to limit themselves and serve the song are invaluable in a worship band. Playing tastefully and discerningly will go a long way to encouraging the congregation to participate. It will also make room for them to be heard.

The rock ensemble is part and parcel of our culture. It's how people celebrate, and I don't think it's going away any time soon. So go ahead and use it, but don't let it rule the gathering. Pull the band out for a song or two, leave choruses open so that voices can be heard. Train your musicians to restrain, restrain, restrain. If your church isn't singing, you're doing it wrong. Period.

Good pastoral leadership will include wise decisions about

songs and dynamics, ensuring that services create space for the congregation to hear themselves, to hear one another, and to join their voices in song. The Psalms manage to describe an enormous diversity in emotions, energy, and instrumentation. All the sections of an orchestra are represented in Psalm 150: strings, brass, woodwind, and percussion; and, of course, breath—not to mention movement to music. With appropriate planning and care, our gatherings can reflect that. Even if they're accompanied by a rock band.

Whatever our preference may be, in the light of Colossians 3:16, a passive, critical, spectator attitude about singing doesn't make any sense. God has brought us into his family and made us a community with one another. He has called us to sing and to testify with our voices, to teach and admonish with our songs about who he is and what he's done. If we fail to participate, we've lost sight of this final point—we aren't acting like recipients of the greatest gift imaginable in the gospel. We aren't singing with grace.

Chip Stam once taught me that worship is a matter of preference and deference. Sometimes I get to sing with my preferences, enjoying the songs, styles, and sounds of music that resonate with my cultural "place." Other times, I defer to others in my church family, joining my voice with their choice of music.

Grace makes that deference joyful. As I join my voice with the diverse community of faith around me, I also join my voice with saints from all of the past two thousand years. Together, we sing and shout, teach and admonish, and experience the rich joy of God's indwelling Word. We sing with grace, and we sing because of grace.

Chapter 10

THE PASTORAL
WORSHIP LEADER

Being a worship leader can be exhausting. We can labor for countless hours, recruiting musicians, coordinating details, thinking
hard about songs, prayers, and Scripture readings in preparation
for a Sunday, and when the day comes, it can still all fall apart. De-
mons in the sound system. Stumbling over words. Songs started
in the wrong key. There can be a constant flow of criticism, and
it sometimes seems like everyone in the church has an opinion
about what we sing and when we sing it.

We're also given conflicting messages about what we're supposed to be doing. We're told over and over again that being a
worship leader isn't about performance, but when we get feedback, it often targets places where the "performance" fell short.
In one breath we're told it's not about us, and in the next we're
thanked for ushering people into the presence of God. We're constantly marketed the latest release from celebrity worship leaders,
and simultaneously told that we're not rock stars.

Defining Priorities
Ultimately, pastors, worship leaders, and church musicians need
a better vision for their task and a clear sense of calling. Instead
of defining that task by what we aren't (we aren't rock stars or
priests), let's define it by what we are: servants given a pastoral
task. John Witvliet says:

As worship leaders, we have the important and terrifying task of placing words of prayer on people's lips. It happens every time we choose a song and write a prayer. We also have the holy task of being stewards of God's Word. Our choices of Scripture and themes for worship represent a degree of control over people's spiritual diets, over how they feed on the bread of life.[1]

Planning and leading worship is a pastoral task. As we step onto the platform on Sundays, we do so as undershepherds of God's church. The songs and prayers we place on the congregation's lips will, to varying degrees, be taken with them into the rest of their week.

This pastoral dynamic should be the defining principle for worship leading. Pastors are meant to be equippers, enabling the church to do its work. In the case of gathered worship, the "work of the people" (the liturgy) is to remember and rehearse the gospel together. We do this as embodied, encultured people speaking to embodied, encultured congregations. The gospel is a message that is constantly on the move, pressing outward from the church and into the culture. People, too, are constantly on the move, being drawn this way and that by the culture around them. Good pastoral work is, in a sense, always the work of a missionary. We seek to understand the culture in which we're immersed and to speak in ways that are comprehensible to that world.

One Pastoral Example

Long ago, a young pastor in training joined his parents for worship in their hometown. He was struck during the singing that the church didn't understand its songs. The people sang almost by rote, and he felt that the language of the songs did more to obscure the gospel than reveal it.

After church, he complained about this problem to his father,

---

[1] Witvliet, *Worship Seeking Understanding*, 282.

who replied, "See if you can do better."[2] That comment sparked the most significant work in the life of Isaac Watts, who is widely considered the father of the English hymn.

Watts's family gathered for worship with an independent congregation, and their worship service involved singing psalms (as was the common practice in English-speaking churches). The translations they used were metered and essentially literal. While they had a precision of language, they lacked beauty, emotive power, and theological clarity. Watts's love for God's Word fueled a pastoral concern: psalm settings should be understandable and should move people to sing in awe of God and the gospel.

Watts's talent as a poet, pastor, and theologian enabled him to make that a reality for generations to follow. He was an innovator, breaking ground in ministry that has continued to impact the church to this day. Even a brief summary of Watts's hymns reveals a breadth of content that stands in contrast with the songs of much contemporary worship music. He wrote hymns of adoration, lament, thanksgiving, and confession; even the imprecatory psalms found a place.

Songs That Sing the Gospel

Watts began his most significant work by resetting the Psalms. As he saw it, Christian worship should be a meditation on the gospel. The practice of exclusively singing psalms had relegated the church's singing to language that was prophetic and predictive, and this excluded the accomplished work of Christ, which illuminates all that the Psalms foreshadowed. So, to put it in modern terms, Watts wanted to write a gospel-centered translation of the Psalms.

> Where [the psalmist] speaks of the pardon of sin through the mercies of God, I have added the merits of a Saviour. Where he talks of sacrificing goats or bullocks, I rather choose to mention the sacrifice of Christ, the Lamb of God. . . .

---

[2] Watson, *The English Hymn*, 162.

Where he promises abundance of wealth, honour, and long life, I have changed some of these typical blessings for grace, glory, and life eternal, which are brought to light by the Gospel, and promised in the New Testament. And I am fully satisfied that more honour is done to our blessed Saviour by speaking His Name, His graces, and actions in His own language, according to the brighter discoveries He has now made, than by going back again to the Jewish forms of worship, and the language of types and figures.[3]

One brilliant example of this is his setting of Psalm 3 (see fig. 2).

Figure 2

Psalm 3, NIV	Psalm 3, Isaac Watts's Paraphrase
[1] LORD, how many are my foes! How many rise up against me!	My God, how many are my fears! How fast my foes increase! Conspiring my eternal death, They break my present peace.
[2] Many are saying of me, "God will not deliver him."	The lying tempter would persuade There's no relief in heav'n; And all my swelling sins appear Too big to be forgiv'n.
[3] But you, LORD, are a shield around me, my glory, the One who lifts my head high.	But thou, my glory and my strength, Shalt on the tempter tread, Shalt silence all my threat'ning guilt, And raise my drooping head.
[4] I call out to the LORD, and he answers me from his holy mountain.	I cried, and from his holy hill He bowed a list'ning ear; I called my Father, and my God, And he subdued my fear.
[5] I lie down and sleep; I wake again, because the LORD sustains me.	He shed soft slumbers on mine eyes, In spite of all my foes; I woke, and wondered at the grace That guarded my repose.
[6] I will not fear though tens of thousands assail me on every side.	What though the hosts of death and hell All armed against me stood, Terrors no more shall shake my soul; My refuge is my God.

[3] Johnson, "The Life of Isaac Watts, D.D.," in *The Psalms, Applied to the Christian State and Worship*, vii.

Psalm 3, NIV	Psalm 3, Isaac Watts's Paraphrase
[7] Arise, Lord! Deliver me, my God! Strike all my enemies on the jaw; break the teeth of the wicked.	Arise, O Lord, fulfill thy grace, While I thy glory sing; My God has broke the serpent's teeth, And death has lost his sting.
[8] From the Lord comes deliverance. May your blessing be on your people.	Salvation to the Lord belongs; His arm alone can save: Blessings attend thy people here, And reach beyond the grave.

To use the modern term, Watts was *contextualizing*. He had a keen ear for language, and he worked as a pastor and artist to help the church understand what they sang. They needed help with language, imagery, and metaphor. They needed to sing the Psalms and see Jesus.[4] Watt's goal was to pastorally exposit the Psalms through song for the sake of building up the church.

This marked only the beginning of the ways Watts would bring reform to worship. In the ensuing years, he would make the argument not only for these theological interpretations of the Psalms, but also for new hymns—new songs written for the church—a change that brought no small amount of scandal itself. In this way, Watts became the father of the English hymn and rightly deserves a place among the greatest names since the Reformation. He paved the way for much of our rich treasury of hymns, and he established the ground upon which our understanding of music's role in the church is seen today. To this day, hymns like "Alas! and Did My Savior Bleed," "When I Survey the Wondrous Cross," and "Our God, Our Help in Ages Past" are sung in churches around the globe. Watts's work inspired Fanny Crosby, author of hundreds of gospel songs, to give her life to Jesus at a revival when she was thirty years old.[5] Henry Ward Beecher in 1872 claimed that Americans' theology was shaped even more by Watts than by the Bible.[6] Watts's three-hundred-

---

[4] Watson, *The English Hymn*, 153.
[5] Petersen and Petersen, *The Complete Book of Hymns*, 954.
[6] Crookshank, *Wonderful Words of Life*, 17.

year-old songs resonate today because of their timeless poetry and theological weight.

Watts's Pastoral Legacy

Interestingly, Watts wasn't a musician. He never wrote melodies for his hymns, instead penning them in meter that could be sung over a variety of tunes (the practice of many hymn writers in his day). His work as a hymn writer flowed from his calling as a pastor and theologian. In our age of celebrity worship leaders and pastors, we can be reminded that Watts was concerned first and foremost with shepherding and encouraging his flock. People don't need a rock star who can wow them with talent; they need a pastor who can help them sing, discerningly choose songs, and craft a culture of worship that effectively promotes the spiritual health of a congregation.

In other words, we need pastoral worship leaders. In our day, many worship leaders stumble into their responsibilities is if by accident. They may be gifted singer-songwriters who fit the cultural mold of the church, are musically talented, and have some character worthy of respect. Without much forethought, they find themselves on staff at the church, the result of being in the right place at the right time. They feel tasked with creativity to keep up with musical trends in worship and keep Sunday mornings vibrant and fresh.

These leaders need to see the call of someone like Watts, who poured his life first and foremost into studying the Word and serving the flock. Only someone with a deep background in the Scriptures and pastoral theology can make discerning decisions about songs, prayers, and rhythms of grace in the life of the church. But because many churches make the gathering simply about music and preaching, the pastoral side of worship planning gets ignored. Songs are chosen because they're musically compelling and inspiring, with little concern about the breadth of our expressions and the way we're building up people's spirituality through song. Music comes first—theology second.

Pastoral Priorities Today

Our challenge today isn't terribly different from Watts's. We need to lead worship in such a way that when people gather, they see Jesus. Like Watts, we need to understand our context and speak creatively to it. Along the way, we need to be willing to boldly challenge tradition for the sake of gospel clarity.

Understanding Our Context

Watts also stands as a brilliant example of pastoral contextualization. His mastery of his language and his culture was put to use helping people comprehend what they were singing. He was willing to buck tradition and risk persecution for the sake of presenting the gospel in a way that was fresh, clear, and compelling.

Today in the church, we wrestle with debates about the limits of contextualization. In the aftermath of the so-called seeker movement in evangelicalism and the current missional movement of church planting, debates swirl about where the lines are between contextualization and compromise, whether by watering down the gospel or by skimping on doctrine.

For Watts, those lines are clear. Rather than assume that the congregation comprehends how the Psalms point to the gospel through their references to kings, enemies, and victories, Watts made those references explicit. His work is resonant in the words of Tim Keller:

> [Worship] language should be free from technical jargon, and especially evangelical subculture terminology. There are innumerable phrases that we fall back on because they sound "spiritual," but they are sentimental and undecipherable for non-initiates. For example: "Let us come *unto* the Lord." "Let us just *lift up* the name of Jesus." "We pray for a *hedge of protection* around him, Lord." Overuse of the word *blessing* is another example of jargon. Key theological terms like *justification* can be introduced and explained. Subcultural talk, however, is at best

highly exclusionary and at worst very phony, a ruse to hide a lack of actual heart engagement.[7]

Our tendency, as Keller points out, is to burden our language (both spoken and in songs) with jargon and terminology that outsiders don't understand. As Watts saw, often insiders don't understand it either. Assumed language in worship will inevitably lose insiders and outsiders. Outsiders hear unexplained theological language and subcultural Christianese and tune out. Like visitors to a foreign country who don't speak the language, they feel alienated and left out.

Christians who have been in the church for years will pick up the lingo, but often their grasp is only skin-deep. We can parrot a whole lot of lofty sounding Christian phrases and never once say anything heartfelt, even when we laden our words with "brothers" and "blessings."

Laboring to explain terms and make concepts clear pays dividends in allowing the church to fully comprehend and thus fully participate in what's being said and sung. Doing this also requires significant legwork from pastors; to speak to our context, we have to understand it.

Three Ways to Think about Contextualization

Contextualization begins with ourselves. The fact is, we are enculturated, embodied persons, and no matter what we attempt to do, we will be enculturated and contextualized people doing it. If I choose to wear vestments and shake a smoking censer in a seven-hundred-year-old cathedral, I will be a thirty-something American doing so. My past shapes my present and how people perceive me. We inescapably bring our personalities and our personal histories with us into our gatherings.

We're also shaped by the history that precedes us. No one since Abraham can honestly claim to have discovered the faith.

---

[7] Timothy J. Keller, "Reformed Worship in the Global City," in Carson, *Worship by the Book*, 225.

(Even Abraham can't really claim that, since God is the one who gave him the promises.) When we gather with the church, we stand in a stream of history, both with Christians who have gone before us and with those who will come after us, whether emerging generations of believers or yet-unreached people in the communities where we gather.

With that stream of worshipers in mind, here are three questions to ask about contextualization.

Who Is Here?

The first question is, who is here? We need to be aware of who already is present in our churches. I've seen many churches aim for a particular cultural vision ("we want to reach urban African Americans") while seeming completely unaware of who they themselves were (white, middle-class suburbanites). This is problematic on two levels.

First, it poorly serves the body of Christ that is already gathering. The members of any church are not merely a means to an end—a team to gather another group for worship. They are the body of Christ themselves. Pastors and church planters are called to shepherd and serve that body, and although preparing the body for its mission is certainly a part of that work, if our contextualization goals fail to factor in the culture of the people already gathered, we dishonor them, placing cultural roadblocks in their path to service.

Second, in most cases, forgetting our own culture poorly serves the target community. There's nothing worse than a poor imitation of a culture's beloved music and language. Bridging cultural gaps requires reaching leaders from within the target culture, empowering them, and letting them lead the way. It doesn't mean "faking it 'til you make it" stylistically. The lack of authenticity and excellence will do far more harm than good. Rather than faking a musical style that is inauthentic, we should focus on trying to draw out excellence from those already serving. Excellence is, to some extent, culturally transcendent. Though an individual may not love gospel music, a truly excellent performance will none-theless be engaging.[8] That's the nature of great art and music—it collects and gathers people who are both familiar and unfamiliar.

The main thing culturally is to know who you are and who your congregation is, and seek to empower them to sing and cel-ebrate the gospel in a way that connects with who they are. If your church looks like a NASCAR fan club, it should sound like a NASCAR fan club when people talk and sing. Don't try to force the church into being something it isn't.

On this topic, I know many worship leaders who cringe at the thought of incorporating one of CCM's big "hits" (I often cringe myself), but we need to think about who our church actually is. Do the people listen to those songs? If so, they're ready to sing them in worship—they've been listening and preparing all week! Is it worth incorporating one or two of those songs in our gather-ings to serve people who are encouraged and blessed by their style and substance?

Who Was Here before Us?

The second question is, who was here before us? This question has a broad range of considerations. If you're pastoring a church with a long history, get to know that history. What did previous gen-erations love and appreciate? How can you celebrate the heritage of God's people who gathered and paved the way for you?

Consider as well the much broader question of the historic church. How are you recognizing that the church didn't start with us? That we stand as part of a tradition stretching across the ages and across international borders?

This isn't to say that you need to start singing in Latin or that you need to sing only historic hymns and chants. But it may be worth incorporating—on a regular basis—some things from out-side your cultural and generational tribe: a creed, a hymn (perhaps even one that's pre-Reformation!), a song from the global church.

---

[8] Keller, "Evangelistic Worship."

Who Isn't Here (and Needs to Be)?

The final consideration is, who isn't here (and needs to be)? This question requires much more prayerful imagination.

- Whom are we trying to reach with the gospel?
- What would it look like for them to wake up one day and start singing songs to Jesus?
- How does this community celebrate in the rest of their lives (weddings, sports events, block parties, etc.)?
- How does this community mourn or lament?
- What would it look like for this community to confess and repent?
- What would it look like for this community to share comfort and assurance?
- What kind of language do they use?
- What is their common level of education, and how should that shape our language?

In North America, speaking to our post-Christian culture takes some serious wrestling. Decisions about the kinds of language we use or about dress, music, and architecture have a great impact on mission, sending signals almost immediately of whether or not a visitor belongs. That's the nature of enculturation; as we speak others' language and paint a picture of the gospel that they can comprehend, we say, "The kingdom has advanced even here."

Contextualization and Modern Music

Music is decidedly cultural. There are very few forms of music that are culturally inclusive—perhaps the national anthem and a few popular folk songs and hymns—but for the most part, the moment you start playing music you begin including and excluding people in the audience.

Our musical preferences often reflect a sort of cultural self-definition. Fans of country music often shop at certain stores, wear certain clothes, and share a certain amount of dialect. The same is true for fans of hip-hop and indie rock. If you take someone in a cowboy hat, snakeskin boots, and a western shirt and drop him in a room full of tattooed, pierced, hardcore kids, he's going to feel like a fish out of water (and vice versa).

For the last twelve years or so, "worship music" has been its own musical style, a sort of quasi-Britpop sound pioneered by British artists like Delirious, Matt Redman, and other Kingsway artists. Somehow, the good work those men and women did in writing songs for their context became "canon" (the rule) for everyone else. Now people hear it and say, "It sounds like worship"—a strange idea, given the biblical story of worship. For those who don't culturally identify with that sound, it's alienating.

When worship gets married to a particular style of music, the consequences are huge. In previous generations, the marriage was between worship and classical music. In my own generation, it's a marriage between particular styles of pop music and worship.

Biblically speaking, there's a better way. One day, every tribe, tongue, and nation will be before God's throne. I think that will include classical music, modern worship, hip-hop, Qawwali folk music, and more. Our churches have the opportunity to be a microcosm of that reality.

Years ago, I spent time helping with occasional services at another church in my city. The worship leader would pick four songs for the service, all of which were four-on-the-floor driving Britpop songs in the key of G. The band begrudgingly pounded through these songs week in and week out, itching for an opportunity to do something different. The other men in the band were ten to twenty years older than I and had been playing music since they were kids. During an occasional rehearsal, when the leader was out of the room for a few minutes, they'd tear into a tune by Van Morrison or Billy Joel, and everyone would roar to life. The piano suddenly sounded "like a carnival," and they rolled through the song with all kinds of passion. Why couldn't they play like that on the other songs? Because they were under orders to replicate a style and a voice that had been marketed (quite successfully) as "worship." Anything else didn't "sound like worship."

I look back on that group of men as a tragic missed opportunity. Musically, there was a lot of firepower in that band. Had they been given a bit of freedom and a little encouragement, they could have translated the songs and hymns of that church into something culturally much closer to the heart of that community. Instead they were handed CDs and told, "play this" because that was what worship was supposed to sound like.

Musical Style and Hospitality

I think of musical style and stylistic diversity as a hospitality issue. When someone walks in the door of our church, what we do musically goes a long way toward making him or her feel included or excluded. If we limit ourselves stylistically to the Christian subculture, then we tell those who don't feel comfortable in that world that they aren't welcome. This goes beyond music, of course, and includes the way we dress, the way we welcome one another, and much more, but music plays a crucial role.

Take classical music, for example. In a context like Midtown Manhattan or downtown Washington, DC, where the church is trying to serve a highly educated, upper-middle-class congregation, classical music connects with the educational and cultural traditions of the community. In the rural South, or in the suburban Midwest, classical music can seem pretentious or out of touch. Likewise, folk and popular music might connect well in rural or suburban contexts, but in a culture that attends the opera and the symphony, it would feel like a youth group.[9]

So what's the best way to navigate these decisions in a local church? Listen. Listen to the people God has gathered. Pay attention to what kinds of music they're listening to and the ways they're celebrating. Pay particular attention to the musicians in the congregation, and look for ways to empower them to play music in styles they love and naturally gravitate toward. Passionate musicians playing in a style they love are always going to be more engaging than a band begrudgingly copying the sound of a hit CD.

---

[9] I heard Tim Keller expound on this a bit at the Gospel Coalition colloquium, May 2012.

I have enjoyed seeing the artists at Sojourn give birth to a variety of sounds and styles. On a given week, you might hear Americana, indie rock, bluegrass, jazzy folk, or straight-forward pop. It's a fairly accurate picture of the musical world of our congregation, and it's our own little preview of that coming day before God's throne, when a diversity of tribes and tongues will sing to the Lord.

Most churches are going to have a stylistic center based on the predominant demographic of the congregation. That should be where a church roots itself musically, but it shouldn't merely stay there. It should also stretch to reflect whatever degree of diversity is present in the church. Musical diversity opens the door to those who are present yet feel on the outside. It also teaches a congregation to not be overly dependent on a musical style for their participation. This goes back to the quote from Chip Stam in a previous chapter—cultivating an attitude of preference (sometimes music is in a style I love and resonate with) and deference (sometimes it's in a style more beloved by others in my church family, and I joyfully defer to them and join them in singing nonetheless).

Worship Should Be Concerned with Both Truth and Beauty

Watts was the consummate pastoral artist. He found the English psalm settings by his contemporaries to be wanting not only for their lack of clarity, but also for their lack of beauty. That he often wrote about the power of poetry to stir affections serves as a reminder that worship should be concerned with both truth and beauty. The psalms themselves were magnificent poems. New Testament hymns like Colossians 1:15–20 and Philippians 2:5–11 and the book of Revelation too are beautiful and poetic. Their authors clearly wanted to light up imaginations as well as communicate facts.

The work of a pastor—whether you're a worship leader or a preaching pastor—calls for a vibrant imagination and creative skills. Creativity isn't simply about saying something new, but about saying it *newly*. A jazz musician, for instance, may never write an original tune, but will certainly give each tune a personal stamp and a sense of originality. Worship leaders, as communicators, have a great challenge before them. Contextualizing the gospel calls for creativity: fresh language, fresh images, fresh ways of saying familiar truths.

As Debra and Ron Rienstra say in *Worship Words*, "One of our tasks as worship leaders, then, is to make the old metaphors come alive again—and to find new ones, too, that fit with the old ones but also keep them renewed and fresh."[10]

Fortunately, God has made us incurably imaginative and creative people. Unfortunately, we're often shy about using that creative energy in the church. Familiar language is safe, and unfamiliar language and metaphors might be misunderstood. We stick with jargon and church-speak because it's comfortable.

Meanwhile, in the world at large, imagination and creativity are relentlessly employed in soul-destroying ways. This is the effect of much advertising, where everything from a sports drink to a Lexus seems to promise soul satisfaction. Some of the best and brightest minds in the creative marketplace are at work trying to figure out how to help you see their product as the solution to your deepest problems. The log described in Isaiah 44 remains a log until the power of imagination makes it an idol to which the carpenter says, "Save me!" All the advertiser needs to do is get a hook in your imagination, and a product becomes a god. To quote James K. A. Smith again, "When our imagination is hooked, *we're* hooked."[11] Then we find ourselves fantasizing about our idols.

The "Expulsive Power of a New Affection"

In some ways, it's easy to recognize our idols. Removing them is another story altogether. As Thomas Chalmers points out in his classic sermon, what we need is a vision of truth that displaces

---
[10] Rienstra and Rienstra, *Worship Words*, 120.
[11] Smith, *Desiring the Kingdom*, 54.

our obsession and affection for these hollow daydreams. He calls it the "expulsive power of a new affection."[12]

Chalmers argues that we can't simply destroy our idols; or to put it another way, we can't simply erase our daydreams. Instead, we must replace them. He says, "What cannot be thus destroyed, may be dispossessed—and one taste may be made to give way to another, and to lose its power entirely as the reigning affection of the mind."

This is why creativity matters. Creatives all around the world are already working to capture people's imaginations. But their goal is to win them over to a political worldview, a clothing brand, or a sports drink.

Our God knows creativity well. As important as doctrine is, as important as legal language and clear facts are, God knows we need our imaginations to be captured by truth. We need to be won over by the surpassing beauty of Christ, the utterly compelling glory of God. We must see these as a greater good and a better hope than all the promises of our idols and daydreams.

So God doesn't merely present the gospel to us in a contract. He gives us a wonderfully creative book in the Bible and invites us to engage with our imagination. Israel's rescue from slavery is both history and allegory. So see yourself in slavery, in the wilderness, and in the Promised Land. The book of Esther is a literary masterpiece, full of irony and wit, telling a story in which God is the hero though his name is never mentioned. The prophets speak to a context that is both particular and universal, inviting us to imagine ourselves in their audience. Likewise, notice how Jesus teaches or responds to theological questions. He often says, "Let me tell you a story. There were once two brothers . . ." or "Two men worked in a field . . ." or "Some young women were waiting on a bridegroom. . . ." He knows that his hearers need more than a black-and-white answer. They need something that ignites their imaginations.

---

[12] Chalmers, "The Expulsive Power of a New Affection."

Full Range of Human Emotion

Throughout the Bible, God sets his sights directly on our imaginations, and we would be wise to follow suit. My friend Kevin Twit regularly talks about how the work of preaching and worship is to present Jesus as more beautiful and more believable to us than he was before. This is one of the ways that creative people can be a profound blessing to the church. It sometimes involves disrupting and disturbing our imaginations—replacing hollow daydreams about status and fame with dreams of a kingdom that turns status on its head, dreams of a rock cut out without human hands that smashes all of our kingdoms and becomes the center of the world (Dan. 2:34).

A little creativity can help to turn the imagination away from the promises of our idols and toward promises and hopes that will never fade. Fresh metaphors can confront and disturb, disrupting the comfortable apathy in which many of our religious thoughts reside, haunting us like Jesus's parables. A song, a story, or even a fresh illustration in a sermon can be tossed alongside us like an innocent gift, an unnoticed package. But inside is a pipe bomb of truth, a mustard seed (to change the metaphor) that can explode in our minds as it takes root, transforming our daydreams from hollow fantasy to faith-invigorated hope.

If we nurture that creativity, it will pay dividends as we seek to lead our churches. For Watts, his immersive education in poetry, cultivated from his childhood, paid off as he set to paraphrase the Psalms and write hymns. The apostle Paul's fluency in Roman culture and religion led him to communicate clear word images to his hearers and readers (Acts 17:16–28; Phil. 3:20). Jesus himself taught in parables that were loaded with imaginative stories and rich imagery. This is why pastors and theologians like Eugene Peterson, David Powlison, and Russell Moore advocate that pastors immerse themselves in literature. Great wordsmiths will help inform our own use of language.

Music, too, provides a tremendous opportunity for creativity.

If our priorities are aligned properly, then our decisions about music will be driven by our desire to love, serve, and nurture the church, and not merely by the adrenaline-inducing effects of certain songs. In our journey through the liturgy's emotional heights and depths, music accompanies us through adoration and lament, confession and assurance, painting the text with tone and tempo and texture. The fact that there is no established musical "canon"—a strict set of approved tunes for the church—means that the infinite variety available in music can be used to present and re-present ideas and their emotional corollaries over and over. We can ever sing a new song because music is so deeply variable.

Breaking Through with Language

For pastors and worship leaders in particular, targeting the imagination requires a ruthless attention to detail regarding language. We need to comb over every word, spoken and sung, continually asking whether people will understand and ideas will be freshly heard.

Language includes and excludes, illuminates or confuses. Great preachers and communicators are language masters, and they rarely let a word slip past them without considering how their congregations will understand it.

I love church history, and I love incorporating readings, prayers, and hymns from those who've gone before us. Occasionally, I think it's a good practice to include something that sounds a little archaic as a reminder that we are part of a long tradition. But for the most part, I believe we need to adapt, edit, and clarify anything we use in our congregational setting for the sake of the church's comprehension. If half the people in the room snicker when someone says, "Here I raise my Ebenezer," then you should probably cut the verse, no matter how much *you* like it. (And very likely, half the room is snickering.)

I remember someone once comparing worship planning to the work of a museum curator: we go into the archives and bring out magnificent, carefully preserved prayers and songs of the church that has gone before us. I tend to think of it as more like the work of a Viking. We plunder the resources of those who've gone before us, hatchets in hand, hacking away anything that isn't clear and helpful in our work of displaying the gospel to the church we're serving. Worship is war, and the Enemy has a million weapons aimed at the hearts and minds of our congregations. His work builds defenses around hearts, wherein people think they know Jesus, think they understand Christianity, but fail to understand the gospel.

We have powerful weapons too, and I think a war-like approach to planning, to making language simple and clear, is necessary if we want to break down cultural barriers to the gospel. That's a key pastoral goal. Gathering for worship is a life-shaping moment in a congregation's week, and our task as pastors is to seize that opportunity for an all-out assault on people's hearts. As servants of God, we prepare people for death, and we prepare them for eternity. And most of them think they're just "going to church."

They gather and they scatter, and what we give them goes with them as they struggle and pray throughout their week. Worship leaders and pastors have been entrusted with the task of building up congregations through the life-giving rhythms of grace. When God's Word is clearly seen, heard, spoken, and sung in worship, hardened hearts are broken, and the weak and browbeaten are lifted up. We are able to join the celebration of the joyful and weep with those who weep. We want to draw out these voices in the songs and prayers of the church in a way that helps worshipers see afresh the story and glory of the gospel.

SAMPLE SERVICE ORDERS

Below are four sample services from churches that, in various ways, are practicing the rhythms of grace. Each one has its own flavor, and I think it's fair to say that many of the differences between them are matters of context. Some of the examples, you'll find, adapt language more aggressively due to the makeup of the congregations, the degree of literacy, and the need for explanation.

You'll see too that there's much in common. All of the services lean heavily on the Scriptures, all rehearse the gospel in the overarching flow of the service, and all sing a mix of hymns and contemporary songs. What's common among them is far more significant than what separates them.

Sample Service from Sojourn Community Church

Note: Words printed in italics are notes for the worship leader. All other type is displayed to the congregation via PowerPoint, and all bold type (except for headings) is read together.

Prelude Song: "Psalm 25," by Joe Day. Copyright © 2000 Joe Day, www.joedaymusic.com. Some rights reserved under the Creative Commons Attribution Non-Commercial 3.0 License.

Words of Welcome: Invitation for newcomers to fill out a Connect Card

Call to Worship
The God who created everything has invited us into his presence. He rightly could demand a laundry list of tasks for us to accomplish or a school of

spiritual merit badges to earn before coming before him. Instead, Jesus offers this invitation:

"Come to me, all you who are weary and burdened, and I will give you rest. Take my yoke upon you and learn from me, for I am gentle and humble in heart, and you will find rest for your souls. For my yoke is easy and my burden is light." (Matthew 11:28–30, NIV)

Today we gather as exhausted, broken, and imperfect people who are being offered rest by a holy God. Let us worship in the open air of his welcoming grace as we stand and sing together!

Song: "Come Ye Sinners." Words by Joseph Hart. Music by Matthew Smith. Copyright © 2000 detuned radio music (ASCAP). Used by permission. All rights reserved.

Song: "Invitation Fountain," by Michael J. Pritzl. Copyright © 2000 Mercy/Vineyard Publishing.

Call to Confession
Pray with me:

Lord, you have opened your arms to welcome us as your children. You alone can forgive our sin. You alone can mend the scars of our shame. When we were found guilty, the blood of your perfect Son, Jesus, was spilled so that we could be declared innocent. Lord, thank you for your mercy toward us.

> **May we run to no other source of refuge.**
> **May we wash in no other fountain.**
> **May we receive from no other fullness.**
> **Or rest in no other relief than in the cross of Jesus our Savior.**
> **Amen.** (adapted from a Puritan prayer)

Let us continue to acknowledge the source of our hope as we sing:

Song: "The Water and the Blood." Words by Isaac Watts. Music by

Neil Robins and David LaChance. Copyright © 2011 Sojourn Community Church.

Assurance/Peace
Hear the good news:

We have been made holy through the sacrifice of the body of Jesus Christ once for all.

> This is God's gospel promise:
> to forgive our sins and give us eternal life
> by grace alone because of Christ's one sacrifice finished on
>   the cross. (see Hebrews 10:10; Heidelberg Catechism,
>   Q&A 66—*The Worship Sourcebook*, p. 123)

As those welcomed and given peace by God, let's welcome each other.

Giving
Hear the words of Jesus:

"Freely you have received, freely give." (Matthew 10:8, NIV)

As an act of worship, in response to God's mercy, we give back to him what he has blessed us with so this church can continue to lift up the name of Jesus in this city and throughout the world. Let's pray:

> *Blessed are you, O Lord our God, Maker of all things.*
> *Through your goodness you have blessed us with these gifts.*
> *With them we offer ourselves to your service and dedicate our lives*
>   *to the care and redemption of all that you have made,*
>   *for the sake of him who gave himself for us—*
> *Jesus Christ, our Lord. Amen.*

Sermon: "Jesus Prayed, Part 1," John 17:6–19

Communion (led by the preaching pastor)

Song: "Jesus, Savior, Pilot Me." Words by Edward Hopper, 1871.

New tune by Joseph Pensak and Isaac Wardell. Arranged by Isaac Wardell and John Totten.

Song: "The Power of the Cross." Words and music by Keith Getty and Stuart Townend. Copyright © 2005 Thankyou Music.

Preparation for Sending
After his resurrection, right before he ascended into heaven where he is now, Jesus told his disciples this:

"Be sure of this: I am with you always, even to the end of the age." (Matthew 28:20, adapted)

Jesus is with us. Jesus is praying for us, even now. Let's sing of the never-ending, unchanging love of our Savior!

Song: "You Never Let Go," by Matt Redman. Copyright © 2006 Sparrow Records/sixstepsrecords. All rights reserved.

Benediction
As you go, remember that the One who owns the cattle on a thousand hills, and watches after every sparrow, didn't spare his Son to set you free. Go with confidence in the Father's provision, joy in the abundant grace of his Son, and power in his Spirit. Peace be with you.

And also with you.

•   •   •

Sample Service from Capitol Hill Baptist Church

This service comes from Mark Dever, pastor at Capitol Hill Baptist Church in Washington, DC, a historic church that is just blocks away from the Capitol building. This service reflects the historic Free Church tradition beautifully.

Note: Italics indicate the leader's notes. Bold passages (excluding headings) are read together.

Preparatory Music (includes "God of the Prophets")

Scripture on Front of Bulletin: 2 Kings 7:9

We gather this morning to praise God, the Judge.

Welcome

Announcements

Let's take a few moments of silence to prepare our hearts for this time together around God's Word.

Scriptural Call to Worship

> Since, then, you have been raised with Christ,
> set your hearts on things above,
> where Christ is, seated at the right hand of God.
>   (Colossians 3:1, NIV)

The assembly that we make up this morning is a congregation that belongs to Christ. We are constituted a single body together by having the same Lord, and by literally sharing the same Spirit. You'll find printed on page 6 this article from our church statement of faith. Let's read it together now.

Statement of Faith
Article XIII. Of a Gospel Church
We believe that a visible church of Christ is a congregation of baptized believers, associated by covenant in the faith and fellowship of the Gospel; observing the ordinances of Christ; governed by His laws; and exercising the gifts, rights, and privileges invested in them by His word; that its only scriptural officers are Bishops or Pastors, and Deacons, whose qualifications, claims, and duties are defined in the Epistles to Timothy and Titus.

How is it that we have become members of the visible church of Jesus Christ? Because he has won us through his selfless love. Let's sing the next two songs. Let's stand as we sing.

Hymn: "The Power of the Cross." Words and music by Keith Getty and Stuart Townend. Copyright © 2005 Thankyou Music.

Hymn: "Grace Greater Than Our Sin." Words: Julia H. Johnston, in *Hymns Tried and True* (Chicago, IL: The Bible Institute Colportage Association, 1911).

Prayer of Praise (led by an elder)

Every story of redemption in the Bible illustrates and points to that final deliverance that Jesus taught us he would bring. Listen now to these words of Jesus from Luke 21.

Scripture Reading: Luke 21:20–28

Do you live ready for this redemption, expecting his return? Have you lived as a Christian this week? Garrett Kell, one of our pastors here, comes and leads us in confessing our sins to God.

Prayer of Confession (led by a pastor)

Scriptural Assurance of Pardon: 1 John 1:8–9

Do you know what happens when we are forgiven by God? We're at peace with him. As our next hymn, on page 9, says, "'Tis everlasting peace, sure as Jehovah's Name; 'Tis stable as His steadfast throne, For evermore the same." And then our next hymn reminds us of the culmination of our hope on that day when we look into the face of the One who gave himself to save us. Let's sing these next two hymns now. Let's stand to sing.

Hymn: "I Hear the Words of Love." Lyrics by Horatius Bonar, 1861.

Hymn: "The Sands of Time." Words by Anne R. Cousin, 1857.

Pastoral Prayer and Prayer of Petition

Daniel 9:18–19: "Give ear, O God, and hear; open your eyes and see [the need of those that bear] your Name. We do not make requests of you because we are righteous, but because of your great mercy. O Lord, listen! O Lord, forgive! O Lord, hear and act! For your sake, [our] God, do not delay, because . . . your people bear your Name" (niv84).

[Note: This prayer, led by an elder of the church, covers a variety of specific requests. On this particular Sunday, Mother's Day, they prayed for mothers, and for others in authority, including judges, President Obama, DC's Mayor Gray, and lawmakers generally. They continued in praying for those in authority in the church, including their elders, specific church planters and missionaries, and sister churches in the city. They prayed for the gospel to bear fruit in a variety of nations in Africa and the Middle East, and concluded by praying for the gospel to bear fruit in their own congregation, specifically praying for the preaching of the Word for the day. This is a great example of a more or less extemporaneous, particular, pastoral praying that was at the center of many of the nonconformist churches' desire for freedom (see chap. 7).]

Hymn: "Speak, O Lord." Words and Music by Keith Getty and Stuart Townend. Copyright © 2005 Thankyou Music.

Prayer of Thanks

Offertory

Message: "The Gospel Illustrated," 2 Kings 6:24–7:20

Hymn: "How Sweet and Awful Is the Place." Words by Isaac Watts, 1707.

Benediction

Silence for Reflection and Preparation

•   •   •

Sample Service from Veritas Church

This service is from Joe Byler, the pastor of worship and arts at Veritas Church, Columbus, Ohio. It's a great example of gospel dialogue throughout the service, and of putting the words of Scripture into the mouths of worshipers as they hear and respond.

Pre-Gathering Song: "Gifted Response," by Matt Redman. Copyright © 2004 Sparrow Records/sixstepsrecords.

Welcome/Announcements

Reading: "Call to Worship"

> L: Blessed be the Lord! For he has heard the voice of our pleas for mercy.
> C: **The Lord is my strength and my shield; in him my heart trusts, and I am helped.**
> L: Our hearts exult the Lord, and with our song we give thanks to him.
> C: **The Lord is the strength of his people; he is our saving refuge! Praise be to God!** (based on Psalm 28:6–8)

Song: "Doxology." Lyrics by Carl Boberg, 1886, and Page CXVI—Limo Cat Publishing (SESAC) © 2010. Music by Page CXVI and David Wilton—Limo Cat Publishing (SESAC) © 2010 (also references an old Swedish folk song in the public domain). Arranged by Page CXVI and David Wilton—Limo Cat Publishing (SESAC) © 2010.

Reading: "Confession/Assurance"

> L: Lord, we know that Jesus, who knew no sin and whose hands were clean, became sin for us, that we might be called righteous, clothed in white and called your children. But at our best, we are still wretched sinners. We still feel as though we're in rags. Our best prayers are

stained with sin. Even our tears of repentance are full of impurity, and our spiritual life is full of pride and selfishness. Help us to repent of our repentance. Wash our tears, and cover us in your righteousness. Like the prodigal son, we run to a far country, and return home, crying, "Father forgive." In your mercy, you call us your children, and you bring us clean garments. May we live in your righteousness, work in it, share our homes in it, be found in death in it, and stand covered by it when we come before your throne.

C: **May we never lose sight of the sinfulness of our sin, the righteousness of salvation, the glory of Christ, the beauty of your holiness, and the wonder of your grace. We ask this in the name of the One who makes it possible, Jesus Christ, Amen.** (based on a Puritan prayer)

Song: "Christ, or Else I Die." From the Gadsby Hymnal, no. 737. Words by William Hammond, 1719–1783. Music by Drew Holcomb, 2004.

Song: "Be Thou My Vision" (public domain).

Passing the Peace (led extemporaneously)

Preaching of God's Word

Communion

L: Jesus's death brings us life and this meal reminds us that we are fed by Jesus and forgiven because of Jesus.

C: **We rejoice that you have died, have risen, and are now with the Father advocating for us. Amen.**

L: With our money, time, and talent we give generously, knowing that through your Son, Jesus, you have generously given to us.

C: **We rejoice that you have given everything, and we joyfully give everything back to your care. Amen.**

Song: "Rock of Ages." Text by Augustus M. Toplady. Music by Thomas Hasting and Brooks Ritter. Copyright © 2011 Sojourn Community Church.

Song: "I Have to Believe," by Rita Springer. Copyright © 2007 KOCH Records.

Reading—Words of Commitment

> L: What can we say in response to God's generous grace? If God is for us, who can be against us?
>
> C: **He did not spare his own Son, but gave him up for us all. Won't he also graciously give us all things?**
>
> L: Who will bring any charge against those whom God has chosen?
>
> C: **It is God who justifies.**
>
> L: Who is he that condemns?
>
> C: **Christ Jesus, who died—more than that, who was raised to life—is at the right hand of God and is pleading with God on our behalf.**
>
> L: Who shall separate us from the love of Christ? Shall trouble or hardship or persecution or famine or nakedness or danger or sword?
>
> C: **Nothing—neither death nor life, angels nor demons, the present nor the future, nor any powers, nor height nor depth, nor anything else in all creation, will be able to separate us from the love of God that is in Christ Jesus our Lord.** (based on Romans 8:31–39)

• • •

Sample Service from Christ The King Presbyterian Church

This service comes from Bruce Benedict, who serves as the director of worship and community life at Christ The King Presbyterian Church in Raleigh, North Carolina. Bruce is also the founder of Cardiphonia, at cardiphonia.com, which is an excellent resource for worship and the arts.

Song of Ascents: "Lord, Send Out Your Spirit," by Rawn Harbor.

Welcome

Call to Worship
Based on Psalm 105:1–2; Romans 5:5; Revelation 4:8

> L: The love of God has been poured into our hearts through the Holy Spirit who has been given to us; we dwell in him and he in us.
>
> C: **Give thanks to the Lord and call upon his name; make known his deeds among the peoples.**
>
> L: Sing to him, sing praises to him, and speak of all his marvelous works.
>
> C: **Holy, holy, holy is the Lord God almighty, who was and is and is to come!**

Prayer of Adoration

Song of Praise: "The Lord Is King!" Words by Josiah Conder, 1824. Altered by Nathan Partain, 2003. Music by Nathan Partain, 2003, UBP.

Song of Praise: "Come, Holy Spirit, Come." Words by William Gadsby. Music: Copyright © Hiram Ring, 2006.

Prayer of Confession

> L: The Spirit of the Lord fills the world and knows our every word and deed. Let us then open ourselves to the Lord and confess our sins in penitence and faith.
>
> C: **Almighty God, who sent the promised power of the Holy Spirit to fill disciples with willing faith: We confess that we resist the force of your Spirit among us, that we are slow**

to serve you and reluctant to spread the good news of your love. God, have mercy on us. Forgive our divisions and by your Spirit draw us together. Inflame us with a desire to do your will and be your faithful people for the sake of your Son, our Lord, Jesus Christ. Amen.

Silent time of confession

Words of Assurance and Peace
Based on Ezekiel 36:24–28

> L: "I will take you out of the nations; I will gather you from all the countries. I will sprinkle clean water on you, and you will be clean. I will give you a new heart and put a new spirit in you; I will remove from you your heart of stone and give you a heart of flesh. And I will put my Spirit in you and move you to follow my decrees."
> C: **"You will be my people, and I will be your God."**
> L: Friends in Christ: by the power of the Spirit, we are united with Christ and given a new spirit. Live in the joy and peace of that assurance.
> C: **Thanks be to the Father, Son, and Holy Spirit.**

Doxology (sung)
[Note: This liturgy was for Pentecost Sunday, and the following readings were broken up into four different languages, with the text printed in English in the bulletin.]

Scripture Reading for Pentecost Sunday

Isaiah 61:1–4

[Mandarin]
> The Spirit of the Lord God is upon me,
>   because the Lord has anointed me
> to bring good news to the poor;
>   he has sent me to bind up the brokenhearted,

to proclaim liberty to the captives,
   and the opening of the prison to those who are bound;
to proclaim the year of the LORD's favor,
   and the day of vengeance of our God;
   to comfort all who mourn;

[German]
   to grant to those who mourn in Zion—
      to give them a beautiful headdress instead of ashes,
   the oil of gladness instead of mourning,
      the garment of praise instead of a faint spirit;
   that they may be called oaks of righteousness,
      the planting of the LORD, that he may be glorified.
   They shall build up the ancient ruins;
      they shall raise up the former devastations;
   they shall repair the ruined cities,
      the devastations of many generations.

Romans 5:1–5

[French]
"Therefore, since we have been justified by faith, we have peace with God through our Lord Jesus Christ. Through him we have also obtained access by faith into this grace in which we stand, and we rejoice in hope of the glory of God.

[Spanish]
"Not only that, but we rejoice in our sufferings, knowing that suffering produces endurance, and endurance produces character, and character produces hope, and hope does not put us to shame, because God's love has been poured into our hearts through the Holy Spirit who has been given to us."

Sermon: "Keep Moving, Don't Stop," Acts 4:19–31

Song of Response: Come, Holy Ghost." Words: "Veni, Creator Spiritus," attributed to Rhabanus Maurus, ca. 800, translated by Rich-

ard Mant, 1837. Chorus by Ray Mills Music: Bruce Benedict and
Ray Mills, 2005.

Confession of Faith
From the Heidelberg Catechism, Q&As 47, 49, 51, 53

> L: In his divinity, majesty, grace, and Spirit, Christ is not
> absent from us for a moment.
> C: **By the Spirit's power we make the goal of our lives not
> earthly things but the things above where Christ is, sitting
> at God's right hand.**
> L: Through the Holy Spirit Christ pours out his gifts from
> heaven upon us his members.
> All: **The Spirit, as well as the Father and the Son, is eternal God.
> The Spirit has been given to us personally so that by true
> faith the Spirit makes us share in Christ and all his bless-
> ings, comforts us, and remains with us forever. Praise to
> the Father, Son, and Holy Spirit!**
> L: Great is the mystery of our Faith
> C: **Christ has died; Christ is risen; Christ will come again.**
> L: According to his commandment:
> C: **We remember his death. We proclaim his resurrection. We
> await his coming in glory.**

> L: The Lord Jesus Christ on the same night in which he was
> betrayed took bread; and when he had given thanks, he
> broke it, gave it to his disciples, as I, ministering in his
> name, give this bread to you, and said, "Take, eat; this is
> my body which is broken for you; do this in remembrance
> of me." In the same manner, he also took the cup, and
> having given thanks as has been done in his name, he gave
> it to his disciples saying, "This cup is the new covenant
> in my blood, which is shed for many for the remission of
> sins. Drink from it, all of you."

Prayer of Thanksgiving

Hymn for the Lord's Supper: "Come, Thou Everlasting Spirit."
Words by Charles Wesley, *Hymns for the Lord's Supper*, 1743. Music
by Bruce Benedict, 2010.

Missionary Spotlight: Missionaries from Asia (parents of Kathryn and Stephen LeTrent)

Song of Sending/Offering: "May the Grace of Christ." Words by John Newton, 1170. Music: "Come Thou Fount."

Benediction

RECOMMENDED RESOURCES

My Top Ten Must-Read Books on Worship and Liturgy

1. *Unceasing Worship: Biblical Perspectives on Worship and the Arts*, by Harold M. Best
2. *Engaging with God: A Biblical Theology of Worship*, by David Peterson
3. *Worship Matters: Leading Others to Encounter the Greatness of God*, by Bob Kauflin
4. *Worship by the Book*, edited by D. A. Carson
5. *Worship, Community and the Triune God of Grace*, by James B. Torrance
6. *With One Voice: Discovering Christ's Song in Our Worship*, by Reggie M. Kidd
7. *Worship Seeking Understanding: Windows into Christian Practice*, by John D. Witvliet
8. *Christ-Centered Worship: Letting the Gospel Shape Our Practice*, by Bryan Chapell
9. *Worship Words: Discipling Language for Faithful Ministry*, by Debra Rienstra and Ron Rienstra
10. *A Royal "Waste" of Time: The Splendor of Worshiping God and Being Church for the World*, by Marva J. Dawn

Additional Recommended Resources: Websites, Blogs, and Music

- Worship Matters—Resources for Leading Worship from Bob Kauflin.
  www.worshipmatters.com
- Sojourn Music
  www.sojournmusic.com

- Cardiphonia—Bruce Benedict's site is loaded with good resources for worship and liturgy.
  www.cardiphonia.com
- Zac Hicks—Zac is a worship leader in the Denver area and has a great blog with reviews, links to other information, and insights about contemporary worship.
  www.zachicks.com
- My Song in the Night—Articles on worship, with an emphasis on songwriting, from Sojourn musicians Bobby and Kristen Gilles.
  www.mysonginthenight.com
- The Worship Community—The forums on this site can be particularly helpful.
  www.theworshipcommunity.com
- Hymnary—This site, run by Greg Scheer, is a comprehensive resource for hymns and hymn tunes.
  www.hymnary.org
- Doxology and Theology
  www.doxologyandtheology.com
- Sovereign Grace Music
  www.sovereigngracemusic.org
- Indelible Grace Music—IG's site includes the online *RUF Hymnbook*, with demos and chord charts for almost every song.
  www.igracemusic.com
- New Old Hymns—Sandra McCracken's website for her hymn projects.
  www.newoldhymns.com
- Keith and Kristyn Getty
  www.gettymusic.com

Resources for Liturgy

Websites

- The Text This Week—An online resource with Scripture readings, prayers, and a variety of other resources based on the lectionary.
  www.textweek.com
- Cardiphonia—Bruce Benedict's site is full of good resources for worship and liturgy.
  www.cardiphonia.com

- Calvin Institute for Christian Worship—Lots of resources; their symposium is one of the best worship conferences to attend. www.worship.calvin.edu

Books

- *The Worship Sourcebook*
- *The Valley of Vision*, edited by Arthur G. Bennett
- The Book of Common Prayer
- *The Devotions and Prayers of John Calvin*, edited by Charles E. Edwards
- *Voicing God's Psalms*, by Calvin Seerveld
- *The Message*, by Eugene Peterson (Peterson originally began writing his paraphrase of Scripture for the sake of public reading.)

THE SOUND OF (MODERN) MUSIC

Technical Challenges for Audio and
Congregational Singing

Churches that use modern music in their gatherings are perpetually facing battles with sound. Modern music tends to be loud, and
that loudness can dominate the congregation. Music is meant to
be in service of the church's singing, not the other way around,
and many little decisions need to be made to safeguard that sense
of musical priority.

Not long ago, I attended a gathering with a congregation other
than my own, and I thought my ears were going to bleed. The
moment the preservice music began, the congregation collectively
shuddered and stood cringing under the instrumental blast for
the next thirty minutes, until the sermon began. We hoped that
the volume would modulate downward after the sermon, but it
didn't. The preacher left the platform and the onslaught continued. I couldn't resist the temptation to pull out my iPhone and
use an app to check the sound levels. While the app surely isn't
the most accurate measurement, it measured sustained levels well
over 110 decibels, which can be damage-inducing. (By contrast, our
sound engineers at Sojourn are trained to keep sustained volume
at about 90 decibels or below, at which they have varied levels of
success.) The irony of this, of course, is that I was in a traditional
service, and the instrument in question was a roaring pipe organ.

Any time you get into the business of amplifying music—even if you're just talking about voices in a single microphone—you present yourself with challenges for congregational worship. I've certainly been a part of worship services that were too loud (and I've been responsible for some of those), but there is a way to navigate these waters without blowing out eardrums or resorting to an entire band wearing headphones.

All Music Is (at Times) Loud, and Should Be

Many assume only contemporary music is loud. This is simply untrue. While a rock ensemble is capable of painfully loud volumes (and it's easy to get to these levels), so is a traditional ensemble. Symphonic music and pipe organs can peak at the same decibel levels as rock music, with the same potential for lasting damage. You encounter similar risks to your hearing at a performance of Handel's *Messiah* as you do at a Matt Redman concert.

Most hearing damage happens when someone has sustained exposure to loud volumes. Every church should buy a decent, inexpensive SPL meter and check levels periodically from different places in the room. You'd be surprised at the variation from spot to spot.

There should be no doubt that, in the gathering of God's people, there's an appropriate time for loud volume. Gather five hundred souls in a room, get them all singing in harmony, and you'll see that they can get incredibly loud—and they should. The psalmist says, "Shout to God with loud songs of joy!" (Ps. 47:1) and, "Praise him with loud crashing cymbals!" (Ps. 150:5). Worship should invoke the kind of celebratory volume that flows naturally from a crowd. We cheer on athleticism at sporting events; we cheer on skill in the performing arts; we cheer on political speeches when they ring true to us. Likewise, we should respond to God's revelation of himself with culturally appropriate, loud celebrations. In North America, the language of celebration in music is often led by some sort of rock ensemble. You can even see it in national politics when Bill Clinton pulls out his saxophone and Mike Huckabee pulls out his electric bass. It's not surprising, then, that this arrangement has become the standard for how many celebrate in our worship gatherings.

The Difference between Bad and Loud

Music that's described as "too loud" is often more of an issue with harshness than with volume. Imagine the sound of your worship band as though they're running through your car stereo. Turn the bass down. Turn the treble all the way up. Now listen at a normal volume level for four or five minutes. It will make you feel like your ears are going to bleed. In reality, it's probably not dangerously loud. It's just dangerously bad. Music regarded as loud, especially in the church where musicians and techs work desperately to tame volume levels, is often simply harsh, imbalanced sound.

Unfortunately, the problems related to bad sound are often heaped at the feet of musical style. The problem, it's said, isn't a particular application of sound; it's the decision to play contemporary music. That's simply not the case. If we pay attention to the details, good sound is most certainly possible with a rock ensemble.

Bad sound can be sparked at any one of a hundred directions. Each step in the process of making music introduces opportunities to get something into the speakers that just sounds bad. Here's a simplified way of thinking about it. All music gets sent through your church's PA along these steps:

1. Musicians
2. Instruments
3. Sound equipment
4. Sound engineers
5. Room

Let's examine each of these.

Musicians

No amount of money spent on gear can make a bad singer sound good or a bad drummer play in time, or turn an unskilled guitarist into Stevie Ray Vaughan. Your sound is only going to be as good as your players. I've seen great players pick up nightmarishly bad gear and instantly sound amazing, because good players pay attention to their sound, pay attention to their room, and work really hard as a band at building a cohesive overall sound.

It's worth considering how you might develop your musicians. This might mean investing in master classes or private lessons. It might also mean narrowing the number of musicians who perform to feature only those with the ability to create cohesive and pleasant-sounding arrangements. That may sound like a harsh choice, but Sunday isn't about giving people an opportunity to play music together. It's about providing an opportunity for the congregation to gather and sing with one voice.

Instruments

In my parents' generation, churches spent massive sums of money on pipe organs and Steinway pianos. The investment was worth it on a number of levels. First, a quality instrument attracts quality musicians. Second, a quality instrument puts a tool in the hands of a musician that enables a wide range of dynamic expression. For instance, an inexpensive piano has a narrow difference between its quietest, darkest sounds and its loudest, brightest sounds. Fine pianos have a much wider dynamic range, enabling the player with more precision to dial in the emotional mood of the song.

This metaphor extends across the musical spectrum. We're often tempted to piece together equipment for the church band as cheaply as possible. Then we're surprised when the cymbals are unbearably harsh and the bass is never in tune.

The investment in quality is worth it. Good instruments make the musicians' job that much easier and more pleasurable.

In particular, let me advocate for two things: First, buy good cymbals. Cheap cymbals sound like trash-can lids, and they ring with harsh, high-pitched overtones that dominate the sound of an ensemble. If a band sounds harsh, often it's because of the cymbals.

Second, buy some decent, low-wattage tube guitar amplifiers. Look for stuff that's about fifteen watts or less. Any guitarist who thinks he needs more is deluded, unless he's playing stadiums four nights a week. Put the amps on kickback stands pointed away from the congregation (at the guitar player's head) and mic them. This will give guitarists a sound they'll enjoy, an amp they can hear, and an overall volume level that will be tolerable for the rest of the church.

Sound Equipment

I'll keep this simple because there's a lot that could be said about sound equipment. If you make the investment in the first two items above (good players, good instruments) then the sound equipment becomes a much smaller issue. Your goal, at that point, is simply to support what the band is doing. So you need speakers with a good, full range of sound (lows, midrange, highs) and with enough power to run clean.

That second point is quite important. Churches often want to buy the fewest and smallest possible speakers for aesthetic reasons, but good, clear sound requires speakers running below their limitations. A rock ensemble usually requires subwoofers to balance out the low end. (Think of this like using the pedals on your pipe organ.) The more you push a sound system to its limit, the harsher everything becomes and the more distortion you introduce. Invest in a sound system that's bigger and louder than you need. You'll be able to get a full range of sound without pushing it to the limit and distorting. (But you'll need to train your sound engineers not to turn things all the way up.)

Sound Engineers

You can't say enough about the importance of good sound engineers. The person behind the board can make a good band sound bad, and a bad band sound worse. Invest in training your volunteer sound techs, and consider stipends for professionals who attend your church. A good engineer will prevent distractions like feedback and keep the overall levels under control.

Room

Every room has a sound. Cathedral spaces were designed to carry a few voices from front to back. Smack a snare drum in that room and it echoes for eternity. Music venues and movie theaters are heavily treated with sound absorption and dispersion materials, creating a space with just the right amount of resonance. Too much resonance and echo, and the sound becomes chaos. Too little and the sound becomes unnatural.

If you're going to use a rock ensemble in worship, it's wise to treat the room in such a way that it hinders reflections, absorbing sound in chairs, bodies, floors, and walls. Without giving attention to the room, you'll perpetually be fitting a round peg in a square hole.

The best way to do this is to contract with a qualified acoustician. Don't guess at what the room needs, because a bad guess could actually make things worse. (This, sadly, is a lesson I've learned the hard way.)

A Sound That Invites

My friend Kevin Twit, who is the founder of Indelible Grace Music and is quite the electric guitar player, talks about the difference between a sound that comes at you and a sound that invites you in. Much modern music is overwhelming, a sonic assault of sorts. By contrast, there are sounds that invite the crowd to sing along, and it's worth asking in our gatherings, is our sound assaulting or inviting?

WORKS CITED

Abernethy, Alexis D. *Worship That Changes Lives: Multidisciplinary and Congregational Perspectives on Spiritual Transformation.* Grand Rapids: Baker Academic, 2008.

Beale, G. K. *The Temple and the Church's Mission: A Biblical Theology of the Dwelling Place of God.* Downers Grove, IL: Apollos, 2004.

Beeching, Vicky. "My Top Tips on Creating a Set List for Worship." *Women in Worship* (blog). Accessed March 15, 2012. http://womeninworship network.com/2010/12/how-do-you-choose-a-set-list.

Best, Harold M. *Music through the Eyes of Faith.* San Francisco: HarperSanFrancisco, 1993.

———. *Unceasing Worship: Biblical Perspectives on Worship and the Arts.* Downers Grove, IL: InterVarsity, 2003.

Blunt, John Henry. *The Annotated Book of Common Prayer.* London: Rivingtons, 1866. http://books.google.com/books?id=pr5CAAAAYAAJ&print sec=frontcover&source=gbs_ge_summary_r&cad=0#v=onepage&q &f=false

Boulton, Matthew Myer. *God against Religion: Rethinking Christian Theology through Worship.* Grand Rapids: Eerdmans, 2008.

Carson, D. A., ed. *Worship by the Book.* Grand Rapids: Zondervan, 2002.

Chalmers, Thomas. "The Expulsive Power of a New Affection." Manna Christian Fellowship—The Gospel and the Heart of Training. Accessed March 15, 2012. http://webscript.princeton.edu/~manna/rubberdoc/c86 18ef3f4a7b5424f710c5fb61ef281.pdf.

Chan, Simon, *Liturgical Theology: The Church as Worshiping Community.* Downers Grove, IL: IVP Academic, 2006.

Chapell, Bryan. *Christ-Centered Preaching: Redeeming the Expository Sermon.* Grand Rapids: Baker, 1994.

———. *Christ-Centered Worship: Letting the Gospel Shape Our Practice.* Grand Rapids: Baker Academic, 2009.

Clowney, Edmund P. *Preaching Christ in All of Scripture.* Wheaton, IL: Crossway, 2003.

Crookshank, Esther R. *Wonderful Words of Life: Hymns in American Protestant History and Theology.* Edited by Richard J. Mouw and Mark A. Noll. Grand Rapids: Eerdmans, 2004.

Dawn, Marva. "But It." Center for Excellence in Preaching. Accessed March 15, 2012. http://cepreaching.org/archive/mdawn-matthew20.

———. *Reaching Out without Dumbing Down: A Theology of Worship for the Turn-of-the-Century Culture.* Grand Rapids: Eerdmans, 1995.

Driscoll, Mark. *Religion Saves: And Nine Other Misconceptions.* Wheaton, IL: Crossway, 2009.

Galli, Mark. *Beyond Smells and Bells: The Wonder and Power of Christian Liturgy.* Brewster, MA: Paraclete, 2008.

Hamilton, Victor P. *The Book of Genesis: Chapters 1–17.* Grand Rapids: Eerdmans, 1995.

Hunter, Todd D. *The Accidental Anglican: The Surprising Appeal of the Liturgical Church.* Downers Grove, IL.: InterVarsity, 2010.

Hurtado, Larry W. *At the Origins of Christian Worship: The Context and Character of Earliest Christian Devotion.* Grand Rapids: Eerdmans, 2000.

Johnson, Samuel. "The Life of Isaac Watts, D.D." In *The Psalms, Applied to the Christian State and Worship.* London: Bagster, 1827.

Keller, Tim. "Evangelistic Worship." Redeemer Presbyterian Church. Accessed March 15, 2012. www.redeemer2.com/resources/papers/evangelisticworship.pdf.

Kidd, Reggie. "Jesus Christ, Our Worship Leader." reggiekidd.com (blog). Accessed March 15, 2012. http://reggiekidd.com/RK/2011/07/12/jesus -christ-our-worship-leader-worship-leader-marapr-%E2%80%9911.

———. *With One Voice: Discovering Christ's Song in Our Worship.* Grand Rapids: Baker, 2005.

Liesch, Barry Wayne. *The New Worship: Straight Talk on Music and the Church.* Grand Rapids: Baker, 1996.

Lucke, Glenn, and Isaac Wardell. "Is a Worship Service More Like a Concert Hall or a Banquet Hall?" *The Resurgence* (blog). Accessed March 15, 2012. http://theresurgence.com/2011/02/25/is-a-worship-service -more-like-a-concert-hall-or-a-banquet-hall.

Montgomery, Daniel, and Mike Cosper. *Faithmapping: A Gospel Atlas for Your Spiritual Journey.* Wheaton, IL: Crossway, 2013.

Owen, John, and William H. Goold. "A Discourse Concerning Liturgies, and Their Imposition." In *The Works of John Owen.* Vol. 15, *The Church and the Bible.* London: Johnstone and Hunter, 1851.

Park, Andy. *To Know You More: Cultivating the Heart of the Worship Leader.* Downers Grove, IL.: InterVarsity Press, 2002.

Petersen, William J., and Ardythe E. Petersen. *The Complete Book of Hymns.* Carol Stream, IL: Tyndale House, 2006.

Peterson, David. *Engaging with God: A Biblical Theology of Worship.* Downers Grove, IL: InterVarsity, 2002.

Peterson, Eugene H. *A Long Obedience in the Same Direction: Discipleship in an Instant Society.* Downers Grove, IL: InterVarsity, 1980.

———. *Under the Unpredictable Plant: An Exploration in Vocational Holiness.* Grand Rapids: Eerdmans, 1992.

Plantinga, Cornelius, Jr. "A Mark of Grace." Center for Excellence in Preaching. Accessed March 15, 2012. http://cepreaching.org/archive/cplantinga-genesis4-2010.

Rienstra, Debra, and Ron Rienstra. *Worship Words: Discipling Language for Faithful Ministry.* Grand Rapids: Baker Academic, 2009.

Sanders, Fred. *The Deep Things of God: How the Trinity Changes Everything.* Wheaton, IL: Crossway Books, 2010.

Smith, James K. A. *Desiring the Kingdom: Worship, Worldview, and Cultural Formation.* Grand Rapids: Baker Academic, 2009.

Sproul, R. C. "Holiness and Justice." Home—Desiring God. Accessed March 15, 2012. http://www.desiringgod.org/blog/posts/r-c-sproul-session-5.

Steele, Anne. *Poems on Subjects Chiefly Devotional.* London: Printed for J. Buckland . . . and J. Ward . . . , 1760.

Taylor, Justin. "Easily Edified." *The Gospel Coalition* (blog). Accessed March 15, 2012. http://thegospelcoalition.org/blogs/justintaylor/2009/06/17/easily-edified.

Taylor, Justin, and Matt Chandler. "One Year Later: An Interview with Matt Chandler." *The Gospel Coalition* (blog). Accessed June 2, 2012. http://thegospelcoalition.org/blogs/justintaylor/2010/11/01/one-year-later-an-interview-with-matt-chandler.

Thompson, Bard. *Liturgies of the Western Church.* Cleveland: Meridian, 1961.

Tillotson, John, and Thomas Birch. *The Works of Dr. John Tillotson . . . With the Life of the Author.* Vol. 2. London: Printed by J. F. Dove, for R. Priestley, 1820. http://books.google.com/books?id=s_c8AQAAIAAJ&pg=PA443&dq=john+tillotson+hocus+pocus&hl=en&sa=X&ei=xrzGT-fgGoGk9ASIopS6Cw&ved=0CEgQ6AEwAQ#v=onepage&q=hocus%20pocus&f=false.

Torrance, James. *Worship, Community and the Triune God of Grace.* Downers Grove, IL: InterVarsity, 1996.

Van Dyk, Leanne, ed. *A More Profound Alleluia: Theology and Worship in Harmony.* Grand Rapids: Eerdmans, 2005.

Waltke, Bruce K. "Cain and His Offering." *Westminster Theological Journal* 48 (1986). Accessed March 15, 2012. http://faculty.gordon.edu/hu/bi/ Ted_Hildebrandt/OTeSources/01-Genesis/Text/Articles-Books/Waltke _Cain_WTJ.pdf.

Watson, J. R. *The English Hymn: A Critical and Historical Study.* Oxford: Clarendon, 1997.

Watts, Isaac, Samuel Worcester, and Samuel Turell Armstrong. *The Psalms, Hymns, and Spiritual Songs, of the Rev. Isaac Watts, D.D.: To Which Are Added, Select Hymns from Other Authors; and Directions for Musical Expression.* Boston: Samuel T. Armstrong, and Crocker & Brewster, 1823.

Webber, Robert. *Worship Old and New: A Biblical, Historical, and Practical Introduction.* Grand Rapids: Zondervan, 1994.

Witvliet, John D. *Worship Seeking Understanding: Windows into Christian Practice.* Grand Rapids: Baker Academic, 2003.

The Worship Sourcebook. Grand Rapids: Calvin Institute of Christian Worship, 2004.

Wright, N. T. *After You Believe: Why Christian Character Matters.* New York: HarperOne, 2010.

GENERAL INDEX

persecution, 73, 106
Peterson, David, 79
Peterson, Eugene, 120
pluralism, 102
praise songs, 128–29
prayers, 94, 100, 110, 128–29, 142
preaching, 20, 80, 100–101, 110, 112, 143
Presbyterian church, 110
prophecy, 85–86
Protestant Reformation, 108–10, 144, 152
psalm singing, 157–63, 171–74
psalms of ascents, 102–3
psalms of praise, 129
Puritans, 109–10

Rayburn, Robert, 144–45
redemption, 12, 42, 56, 65, 71–72, 75–76, 122–23, 136–38
regulative principle, 20–21
repentance, 58, 97, 112, 123, 161
resurrection, 66–67, 101
revivalism, 111–15
Rienstra, Debra, 118, 127, 183
Rienstra, Ron, 118, 127, 183
Roman Catholicism, 87, 108, 114–15

sacraments, 110
sacrifices, 54–55, 58, 66–67
Sanders, Fred, 26
seeker-sensitive movement, 86, 175
sin, 32–34, 55, 57, 64, 84, 90, 130–31
singing, 161–67, 207–12
Smith, James K. A., 93, 103–4, 136, 145, 148, 183
sound engineers, 211–12
sound equipment, 211
Sproul, R. C., 58
Stam, Chip, 155, 167, 182

Steele, Anne, 160–61
suffering, 46, 65, 81, 132–35

Taylor, Justin, 133
Temple Model, 113
temple worship, 49, 51–54, 69, 79–80, 95
Tolkien, J. R. R., 28
Trinity, 26–27, 30–31, 71–72, 75, 148
Twit, Kevin, 185, 212

vestments, 110
volume, music, 207–9

Waltke, Bruce, 40
Wardell, Isaac, 98–99
Watts, Isaac, 170–76, 185
Webber, Robert, 101
Wimber, John, 113
Witvliet, John, 30, 97–98, 118, 127, 162, 169–70
worship
  audiences of, 82–90
  concert hall versus banquet hall, 99–101
  context of, 76–82, 88–89
  of the Israelites, 49–59, 70–71, 78, 96–97, 101–2, 157
  music in, 153–67
  object and author of, 75–76, 87–88
  orders of, 107, 189–203
  planning of, 170
  as spiritual formation, 91–104
worship leader, 21, 84, 166, 169–88
"worship wars," 74, 86, 92, 103–4, 112, 155
Wright, N. T., 30

Zwingli, Ulrich, 144

SCRIPTURE INDEX

An exploration of the whole gospel for the whole church for the sake of the whole world.

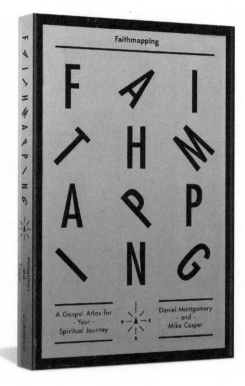

FAITHMAPPING:
*A Gospel Atlas for
Your Spiritual Journey*

"The title says it all! It is a trusted navigator for those who desire for Christ to be all."
DARRIN PATRICK, Lead Pastor, The Journey, St. Louis, Missouri

"This book, full of gospel beauty and Bible wisdom, can light up the path in front of you, as you walk the path God is stretching out before your feet. Read it, and feel the fire."
RUSSELL D. MOORE, Dean, The Southern Baptist Theological Seminary

For more information, visit crossway.org.